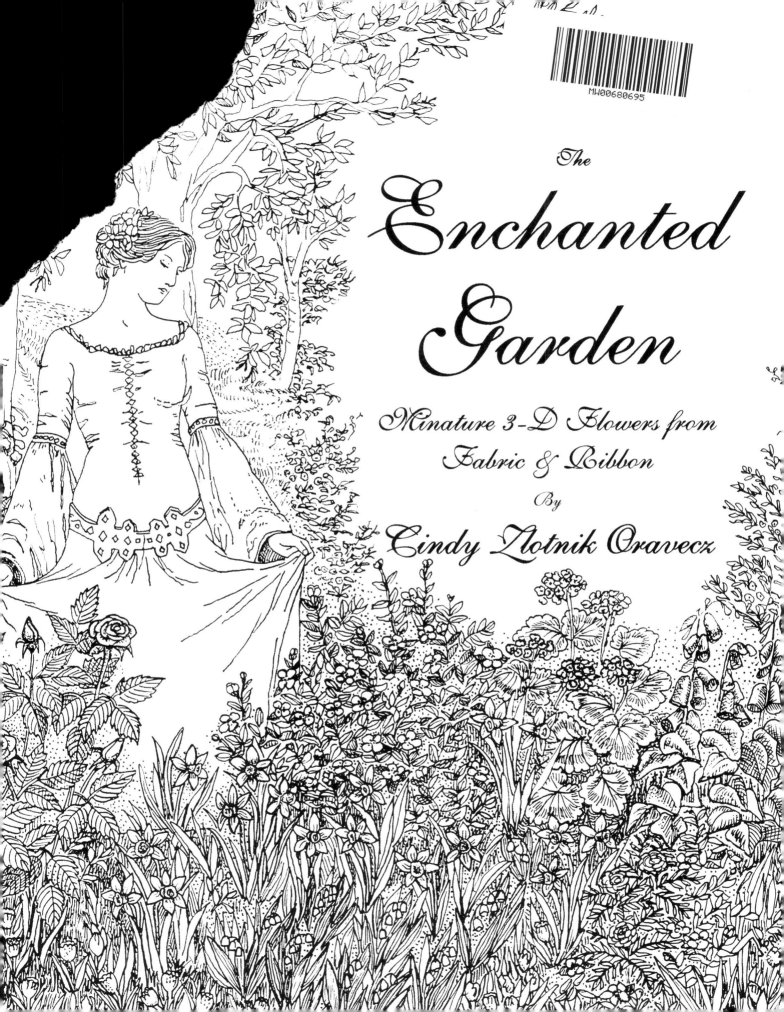

The

Enchanted Garden

Miniature 3-D Flowers from
Fabric & Ribbon

By

Cindy Zlotnik Oravecz

This book is dedicated to my mo

Nadine Zlotnik

for all her love

First Edition, First Printing

Copyright © 1997 by Cindy Zlotnik Oravecz

Published by Quilters Fancy, 137 Winter Lane, Cortland, Ohio 44410-1129. U.S.A.

Printed by Sheriar Press, 3005 Hwy. 17 N. Bypass, Myrtle Beach, South Carolina 29577

ISBN 0-9652160-1-2

Table of Contents

...oduction 5

...asic Guidelines 6

The Flowers 7

Bleeding Heart 7

Daffodil 9

Hepatica 10

Mum 11

Old-fashioned Rose & Begonia .12

Pansy 14

Rosabella 16

Sunflower 17

Wildflower 18

Flower Centers 19

French Knot Center 19

Mad about the Leaf 20

Broderie Perse Leaves 20

Quick Miniature Ribbon Leaf . .21

Templates for Leaves 21

The Album Blocks 22

Friendship's Bond 22

Encircling Peace 24

Petals & Ribbons 26

Daffodil Splendor 28

Welcoming Begonias 30

Sunshine's Joy 32

Love Is 35

Elegant Bounty 38

Spring's Blessing 40

Appliqué 46

The Fine Art of Appliqué and Tranquility 46

Invisible Appliqué: Is It Skill Or Is It Zen? .47

Why Isn't Anyone Talking about Fingernail Pressing 48

Tips For Invisible Needleturn Appliqué from A To Z 48

Borders 52

3-D Swag Border 52

Seminole Border 54

About the Author 55

Resources 56

Acknowledgements

A very special thank you to my husband for his dedication in helping me produce this book, and Michael for their support; to Janice Prince, who created inspiring illustrations with great ze... The Art Farm, who captured the depth of the 3-D textile in photography and Cindy for her kind ho... Lawrence, my printing guru -- she does it with finesse and fun; Peg & Joe Viole for endless support, a... ter; Virginia & Mike Walton, for devotion to the cause; Miriam Oravecz, for support; Judy Shuttic & Fam... Hodges, Lana Eisenbraun, Peggy Adams and Ellie Stewart.

Thanks to Clotilde, MV Designs in Australia, Nancy's Notions, Quilter's Rule, Quilter's Resource, and Roya... Publications for carrying Quilter's Fancy products. And thanks to all the quilters who pick up their needles ever...

Graphic Production by Steve Oravecz

Diagrams & Illustrations by Janice Prince

Photography by Dennis Ryan, The Art Farm

Design Consultation by Sunny Lawrence

Color Processing by Rudinec & Associates, Youngstown

Printing by Sheriar Press, 3005 Hwy. 17 N. Bypass, Myrtle Beach, SC 29577

Introduction

Step Into The Enchanted Garden with me. This is where the tiniest of dimensional flowers grow in an inspiring rainbow of colors. You'll find some of my old favorites from my first book, "Into The Garden," but in a much smaller size.

There is the ever-charming Bleeding Heart, the rolled and ruched Hepatica, silk ribbon stars the Mum and the Pansy, the "u curve" Old-Fashioned Rose and the quick Wildflower.

I've added some new blossoms to the garden. The sunny Daffodil, the Rosabella, the smallest flower of all, and a Sunflower are all growing in miniature as well, as we journey together "Into The Enchanted Garden."

This collection of dimensional flowers contains patterns for nine new 6-inch square quilt blocks. All nine blocks can be combined into one nine-block wallhanging, a four-block wallhanging or a single-block center medallion wallhanging surrounded by borders. The patterns work well on wearables, too.

As usual the instruction includes variations to choose from, so your work can be one-of-a-kind. All the flowers can be made from fabric or ribbon. In addition, the dimensional flowers can be interchanged on the quilt blocks.

One of the favorite classes to grow out of my Flowers Faster By The Strip series is Spring's Blessing. Here in The Enchanted Garden is this surprising basket project in miniature. You'll find two versions, one filled with a fistful of silk ribbon pansies and another just filled to overflowing with a riot of colorful blossoms. This very easy basket can be filled with whatever flowers are your favorites. That means anything goes! And when we step into the realm of anything goes, something gets loose - your creativity.

The quilter becomes the florist. All the flowers are made first. A straight pin can go into the center of each flower as if it were an hors d'oeuvre on a fancy toothpick. Then by simply picking up your flower hors d'oeuvres by the glasshead pins, you can arrange them into a bouquet to your liking. With the help of a few simple design rules, it's exciting to unleash your creativity and see where it leads.

The quilter as florist has the continual challenge of color. Whether you are new to color or just are not comfortable yet handling color, there is a special color dialogue between you and me inside. I like taking the technical terms out of color theory. You'll see how complementary good neighbors can be.

Special attention must always be lauded onto leaves. Could flowers steal the show so magnificently if it weren't for lush g... trasting and supporting t... you, too, will become ``Mad...

The Album blocks are a pro... beginning with the easiest blocks. ... skill, the blocks will challenge you.

When I first began playing in miniatu... admit I felt awkward. My fingers were use... larger quilt blocks. It took me about 30 days to g... thinking and my fingers down to size. But once I di... just fell in love with this size quilt block, and I hope you will, too.

Happy Stitching,

Cindy O.

Basic Guidelines for Using This Book

Block Size: All quilt block patterns are designed for a 6-inch finished quilt square. Cut all blocks 6 1/2 inch square on grain. Decide if you want the quilt blocks to be centered on point or square.

Stitch Size: All flowers are sewed with a hand gathering stitch. The stitch is about 1/8 inch long.

Kind of thread: These gathering techniques require strong, fresh new thread. The thread for gathering the flowers used is an all-purpose weight cotton-covered polyester. Use silk thread only when appliquéing.

Length of thread: The thread is always doubled in the needle. Therefore, if the directions call for a 12-inch working thread doubled, that means to cut the thread 24 inches long. If you need to use a single thread in the needle, you can use a quilting thread. The double thread has the added bonus of insuring that the needle does not get lost. I like to just let the needle dangle. Unless, specified it is important to use an 18-inch length of thread in the needle. This tried and true measurement insures that you do not get knots.

Working board: A working board just slightly larger than the block size is handy for many of the block patterns. To make a working board: cut a 7-inch square of corrugated cardboard. The cardboard must be corrugated — two layers of cardboard with waffle grooves and air sandwiched in between. Totally cover the surface of the board with very thin white or cream batting or white felt. Glue in place.

Embroidery Hoop: When tacking a finished dimensional flower to the background block, always put an embroidery hoop around the area first. This insures that the background block will not be bunched up and distorted from the long tacking stitches. A five- and a six-inch embroidery hoop are needed for these designs.

The Stick-and-Stab Stitch: All the dimensional flowers in this book are stitched down to the fabric with a stick-and-stab stitch which is also called a tack stitch. This is simply a stitch coming from the back of the work up through a fold in the flower. The needle then goes back down though the same fold in the flower just a few threads away. The stitch is taken tightly with a doubled thread in the needle. Many times, to make sure a tack stitch holds extra tightly, knot behind the stitch before taking the next tack stitch.

Appliquéing: The foundation behind album block quilts is appliqué. The ``right'' method of appliqué to use is the one that you personally enjoy. I've included a section on needleturn appliqué and finger pressing because that is the method I enjoy and feel is very easy. But many people who make these dimensional flowers are not interested in appliqué. There are other easy choices available also. I recommend Eleanor Burns' *Appliqué In A Day* methods which include machine sewn appliqué with the use of fusible pellon. Also machine blind hemstitching or other edge stitching is an effective way to appliqué by machine.

Needles: The best needle for gathering is the milliner's needle. In addition to being long, the beauty of the milliner's needle is that it is the same thin width from the eye to the point. This allows the needle to travel more swiftly through fabric or ribbon with less drag while gathering. Milliner's needles size 9 or 10 are recommended for gathering fabric and French Elegance wire ribbon. A straw needle No. 11 is recommended for finer 7 mm silk ribbon.

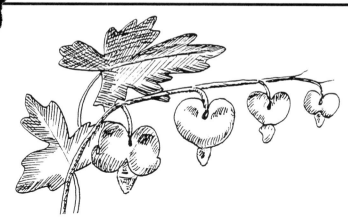

The Bleeding Heart

Bleeding Hearts are arching sprays that drip with heart-shaped flowers with tiny tears. What makes this flower attractive in album blocks is how the lovely puffed-heart shape and color repeat on the stalk. Also the stalk is unusual because it hangs horizontally in bouquets. The horizontal stalk makes a nice contrast in design.

A Bleeding Heart stalk can contain up to 16 blossoms. On album blocks a spray of 5 Bleeding Hearts is sufficient, but add more if you like.

Bleeding Hearts can be all white, or choose a mottled pink fabric for the heart and white fabric for the tear.

MATERIALS:

The miniature bleeding heart comes in two sizes. The small size uses a mottled pink square of fabric just one-inch square. The large size uses a mottled pink square of fabric just 1¼ inches square. Cut the tears from a square of white fabric just 1¼ inches wide by ½ inch. The small tear uses even less than that, just to give you an idea of how much fabric is needed. For precise measurements, see templates in Step 1.

My best recommendation for comfortably sewing the bleeding heart is to choose fabric with a very high thread count per inch, such as a pima cotton. Hoffman Bali fabrics are ideal because the fabrics are swirled with colors perfect for the bleeding heart and have the very dense thread count needed. A looser weave fabric can be frustrating to work with because it will fray.

Thread up two milliner's needles with white thread doubled. Park in a pincushion.

1. Cut bleeding heart templates, Fig. 1-1 and Fig. 1-2. Trace around five-sided template onto pink fabric, adding 1/8-inch seam allowance on all sides. Trace around triangle template onto white fabric adding 1/8-inch seam allowance on all sides.

> **HELPFUL HINT**:
> Remember to mark both plastic pieces of each bleeding heart with the specific size — large or small — so the pieces do not get confused.

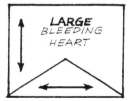

Fig. 1-1

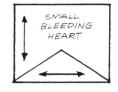

Fig. 1-2

2. Using a doubled white thread, piece the white triangle onto the pink piece. This is called setting in an angle. With *right* sides together, lay the short side of the triangle onto one short edge of the five-sided piece. Sew from corner to center on the pencil line using a tiny running stitch and backstitching every fourth stitch. (This is the hand piecing stitch). Knot but do not cut thread. ***Before sewing other side, slash to "v" on pink fabric only***, as in Fig. 1-3. Sew other side of triangle to corner.

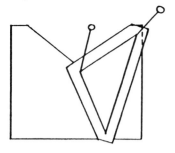 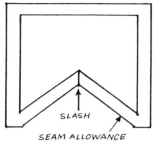

SLASH

SEAM ALLOWANCE

Fig. 1-3

3. Press white triangle seam allowance toward pink fabric. Press or fingernail press 1/8-inch seam allowance on **all four sides** of rectangle toward wrong side. Trim corners near pieced seams.

4. Using washout or brush out pencil, place a dot 1/8-inch above the "v" on the right side of pink fabric, as in Fig. 1-4.

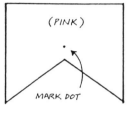

(PINK)

MARK DOT

Fig. 1-4

5. With white thread doubled, gather on the right side of white fabric **in the ditch along the "v", sewing through seam allowances at corners, as in Fig. 1-5.** Pull as tight as possible, pinch the gathers together with thumb and index finger. While pinching gather, make a knot.

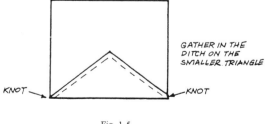

GATHER IN THE DITCH ON THE SMALLER TRIANGLE

KNOT — —KNOT

Fig. 1-5

6. Shape the tear: Turn bleeding heart to back side, pinch the raw edge of tear together with thumb and index finger. Check the front of the tear to see if it looks slender and is shaped properly. Whip stitch back of teardrop together where you pinched the fabric,

catching as many raw edges as possible. (Any stray raw edges will be tucked under and appliquéd to ground fabric later.)

7. With white thread doubled, gather just 1/16 inch from folded edge (through seam allowance) starting at bottom corner where pink meets white. Gather around in heart top shape **through seam allowances** and down to other side where pink ends, as in Fig. 1-6.

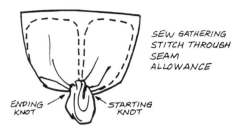

SEW GATHERING STITCH THROUGH SEAM ALLOWANCE

ENDING KNOT   STARTING KNOT

Fig. 1-6

Pull gathers snug enough so that edges cup under and the curved heart top forms.

8. Take time to slide a point turner or other blunt tool inside the heart to poke the puckers outward making the heart nicely shaped. Appliqué in place.

THE ALL WHITE BLEEDING HEART

For all white or cream bleeding hearts simply trace the whole rectangle template, add 1/8-inch seam allowance and mark in brush out pencil "v" to gather on. There is no need to add the triangle piece. Finish as old-fashioned bleeding heart.

BLEEDING HEART PLACEMENT

The bleeding hearts arch gracefully on an imaginary horizontal line. For the Spring's Blessing, the bleeding hearts lie tucked under other flowers, so no stalk is needed.

1. First, line all the hearts up in order largest to smallest. The largest hearts will be at the center of arrangement or the basket and the smallest heart will trail at the outside tip of the stalk. Remember that the hearts grow largest to smallest on the stalk.

2. Place bleeding hearts so that the first tiny heart on the end of the stem is on the same imaginary horizontal line as the last largest bleeding heart radiating from the center of the flower arrangement. (Leave space between for the other bleeding hearts).

3. Now fill in with the remaining three hearts, which arch up between the beginning and ending hearts.

VARIATION: Another arrangement for the stalk can be for the largest center bleeding heart to be at the highest point in the center of the basket with the remaining four hearts trailing downward.

The Daffodil

Daffodils can be created in many stunning color combinations today. Daffodils can have white or cream petals with light coral, pink, apricot, yellow or orange centers. Just how pale or deep the centers is in color affects the look of the daffodil greatly. Many different tones of yellow can be combined as well in petals and centers. Centers of yellow-petal daffodils can also be orange.

DIRECTIONS

1. For each daffodil: Cut 5 circles each 1 1/8-inch in diameter, as in circle template in Fig. 1-7.

NOTE: This is the same circle template used to make the sunflower.

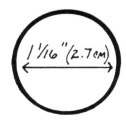

Fig 1-7

2. Fold each circle in half and finger press or iron crisply. Then fold each half in half one more time to form a quarter pie wedge, as in Fig. 1-8.

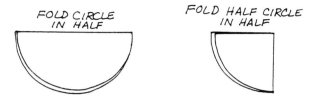

Fig. 1-8

3. With a doubled thread in matching color, gather about 1/8 inch (no more) from raw edge, as shown in Fig. 1-9. Stitches should be about 1/8-inch long — no shorter. Pull the gather as tight as possible. KNOT — BUT DO NOT CUT THREAD.

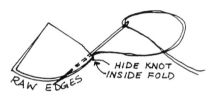

Fig. 1-9

HELPFUL HINT:
To pull a gather as tight as possible, try this: Pull gather as tight as possible pulling the thread near the fabric, pinch the gather between index finger and thumb. While holding gathers pinched tight, relax the thread and knot.

4. Gather next folded circle petal onto the same thread. Gather. Pull thread as tight as possible. ***KNOT — BUT DO NOT CUT THREAD.***

5. Repeat gathering and stringing for the remaining three petals on the thread, as in Fig. 1-10.

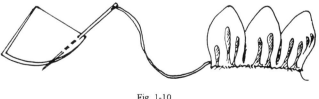

Fig. 1-10

6. Butt raw edges of last petal and first petal together to form petals into a circle so petals form a star.

7. Cut a one-inch square of crinoline.

8. Tack daffodil petals onto crinoline with a stick-and-stab stitch in petal folds in as small as possible circular shape, as shown in Fig. 1-11. To keep star circle small, push all petals toward center while tacking to keep inner hole as small as possible.

Fig. 1-11

MAKE DAFFODIL CENTER

1. Each daffodil center is one miniature mum tacked over the completed daffodil petals. Follow steps 1 through 9 for Mums on pages 11-12 to make daffodil center. Tack the mums at the center of the star of petals, covering the raw edges, as in Fig. 1-12.

Fig. 1-12

Hepatica

MATERIALS:

• French Elegance wire ribbon 5/8 inch wide in gradated shades of maroon. French Elegance wire ribbon 5/8 inch wide in red wine to butternut.

• A sharp chalk marker like The Chalk-o-liner from Clover Needlecraft — **or** — a sack of powdered marking chalk like The Pouncer.

• The Mini Ruching Edge

DIRECTIONS:

1. For each Hepatica, cut red wine to butternut yellow ribbon 1¼ inch long.

2. Cut maroon ribbon 7 inches long.

3. Piece smaller ribbon to larger ribbon with a 1/8-inch seam allowance, being careful to have both right sides of ribbon together, as in Fig. 1-13.

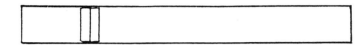

Fig. 1-13

4. Spread a scant amount of washout glue stick along the wrong side of pieced ribbon. Fold entire strip in half being careful to make sure the wire edges of the ribbon are jogged so that they lie neatly next to one another along length of ribbon, as shown in Fig. 1-14.

Fig. 1-14

NOTE: The right side of the ribbon often has more colorful fibers covering the wire. The fibers covering the ribbon on the wrong side of the ribbon are whiter and also lie flatter over the wire.

5. Spread gluestick along just the smaller piece of yellow ribbon and fold this ribbon only in half again along its length.

6. Form the rolled center: Fold beginning raw edge of yellow ribbon on 45-degree angle, as shown in Fig. 1-15. Then roll yellow ribbon toward seam, stopping where the yellow ribbon ends as shown.

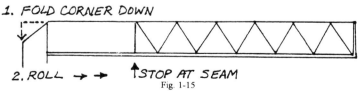

1. FOLD CORNER DOWN
2. ROLL → → ↑STOP AT SEAM
Fig. 1-15

7. Snip off any tail that forms at the bottom of the rolled center.

8. Using matching thread, whipstitch rolled center bottom in place with 3 or 4 stitches.

9. Using a sharp chalk marker, mark the lighter side of the maroon ribbon with The Mini Ruching Edge beginning with ½ of a "V" at the seam and rolled center top, as shown in Fig. 1-16.

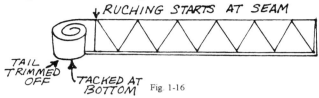

Fig. 1-16

10. Using a doubled, all-purpose thread, gather on lines beginning at seam and gathering to raw edge. Take 3 to 4 stitches across each diagonal line and pull stitches as tight as possible as you stitch.

NOTE: Finished gathered ruched ribbon only should measure 1 7/8 inches from seam of yellow ribbon to end of ruching. Do not count the raw edge tail that will be tucked under the ruching in this measurement. Knot off.

11. Spread ruched gathers evenly.

12. Cut a one-inch square of crinoline.

13. Swirl ruched petals around center on crinoline.

NOTE: Tail of ruching covers beginning first hump of ruching near rolled center or a bit more if needed. Just tack stitch overlapping ribbon firmly in place.

14. Using one straight pin, pin beginning and end of ruched petals together. Tack the flower onto the crinoline: Using a matching doubled all-purpose thread, tack petals in place hiding stitches in folds surrounding rolled center. Knot at back.

15. Using a matching doubled thread, tack rolled center in place through crinoline drawing the center down firmly in the flower, as in Fig. 1-17.

Fig. 1-17

16. Position five flowers on wreath as in the color photo of the Ribbon Wreath (more if you prefer) and poke pin in place.

The Mum

This miniature flower is intriguing to look at because the tiny scallops and folds create texture on the surface of the quilt block. The mum is equally beautiful made from fabric or ribbon.

MATERIALS:
For each flower use either:

• 5 inches of 3/8-inch-wide (7 mm) silk ribbon — **or** — a straight grain strip of fabric 5/8-inch wide by 5 inches long.

• A sharp chalk marker.

• The Mini Ruching Edge

DIRECTIONS:

1. If using fabric, press raw edges so they meet at center back as shown in Fig. 1-18. Use any lightweight fabric that can be ironed and will hold a crease, such as cotton, silk or rayon. Metallics can even be used, but use a press cloth to prevent melting the fabric. There is no need to fold ribbon.

Fig. 1-18

HELPFUL HINT:
Spray fabric with spray starch before pressing because the crisper the fabric is pressed, the easier it is to ruche.

2. Place zigzag edge of The Mini Ruching Edge so its peaks just reach top of strip and valleys touch bottom.

3. Mark around zigzag edges onto strip with chalk marker as shown in Fig. 1-19, or glide The Pouncer across the entire zigzag edge to quickly mark all zig-zags in one stroke.

MEDIUM RUCHE

The Mini Ruching Edge ™

Fig. 1-19

4. Use a No. 9 or 10 milliner's needle for fabric and a No. 11 straw needle for silk ribbon and a doubled regular thread with a working length of 12 inches. Gather along marked lines with 1/8-inch-long stitches, as shown in Fig. 1-20.

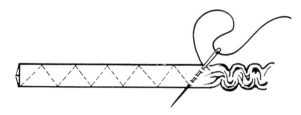

Fig. 1-20

5. Pull gathers as stitching.

6. If using cotton fabric, pull gathers as tight as possible. This will make the finished gathered fabric strip measure 1¼-inch long not including the raw edge tails. Neatly tuck the raw edge tails behind the ruched strip and tack in place. If using silk ribbon, adjust finished gathered strip to be 1/8 inch long after raw edges are tacked behind.

7. Cut a one-inch square of stiff crinoline.

8. With a doubled thread in matching color, use stick and stab stitches to hold one tail in place on crinoline.

9. Butt remaining tail end right up to beginning tail to form strip into one complete circle as shown in Fig. 1-21. Tack petals in place.

NOTE: When tacking flowers in place, take time to spread petals and especially manipulate the soft folds of silk ribbon to make flower full and pretty.

CONNECT TO FORM CIRCLE

Fig. 1-21

Old-Fashioned Rose or Begonia

The old-fashioned rose and begonia are made the same way. The fabric or ribbon choices and the leaves that lie behind the blossom change the look of the flower.

Choose fabric or ribbons that have color gradations blending and swirling randomly throughout. This randomness best captures the realism of flowers.

As with the pansy, this flower can be pieced as well at the junction where each "u curve" meets the next "u curve" on The Mini Ruching

Edge. Always piece with a 1/8-inch seam allowance. In this way, not all of the 9 or 12 petals need to be made from the same color.

Here is an example of a way to piece the strip before gathering the flower:

• *The first two petals could be a light pink. This fabric would be cut ¾-inches wide by 2 1/8 inches. (Each petal is 1-inch wide on The Mini Ruching Edge times 2 petals plus seam allowance.)*

• *The next three petals could be medium pink. This fabric would be cut ¾ inches wide by 3¼. (Each petal is 1-inch wide times 3 petals plus two seam allowances.)*

• *The remaining four petals could be a deep pink. This fabric would be cut ¾-inches wide by 4 1/8 inches. (Each petal is 1-inch wide times 4 plus one seam allowance.)*

Graduating color in this flower from light at the center petals to deeper at the outside petals makes the flower more real looking and more dramatic in the basket or bouquet.

MATERIALS:
• ¾ inch by 9 or 12 inches, whatever size preferred fabric or Artemis bias silk ribbon

• 3/8 inch (7 mm) silk ribbon, either 9 or 12 inches long

• The Mini Ruching Edge

• A sharp chalk marker

DIRECTIONS:
1. This flower can be made from fabric cut ¾ inches wide or from Artemis's ¾-inch wide bias cut silk ribbon (which comes in scrumptious flower-like color blends) or from (3/8-inch) 7 mm silk ribbon. Regardless of what is used, the length of the strip is 9 inches for a regular size miniature flower and 12 inches for a larger miniature flower.

2. If using fabric or Artemis ribbon, first fold the strip in half along length. Other ribbon needs no preparation.

3. Follow steps 2 through 4 for pansy on page 15.

4. When done gathering, do not knot off let the threaded needle dangle. Pull the thread so that the gathered strip will measure exactly 7 inches long from raw edge to raw edge for the regular size flower. The larger flower should measure 9 inches long. Do not worry about adjusting the gathers as yet. Simply knot off.

5. Adjust gathers so that the first two petals formed are gathered tightly. The next three petals should be adjusted looser. The remaining petals are so loosely gathered that they just begin to cup and form petals. Strip should look like Fig. 1-22.

Fig. 1-22

6. Arrange the gathers by coiling the flower in your hand. To do this, begin by laying your thumb or index finger, whatever is comfortable for you, inside the first petal that will be at the center of the flower (with your nail along the raw edge) as shown in Fig. 1-23.

Fig. 1-23

7. Twirl the remaining petals behind this first petal while turning the flower in your hand. The petals do not all lie right behind each other, but radiate outward as the flower is coiled around, as in Fig. 1-24.

13

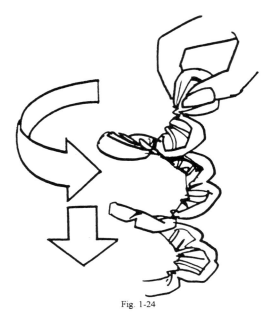

Fig. 1-24

8. Experiment and coil the flower in your hands or on a table as many times as necessary until the flower looks round and balanced, as in Fig. 1-25.

Fig. 1-25

9. When satisfied with the flower, knot off the gathering thread.

10. Carefully turn the flower upside down in your hand and from the back, run a doubled thread through the raw edges that circle around. Travel from one side of the flower straight across catching raw edges. Continue back and forth across the back of the flower, **being careful not to pull thread too tightly**, but merely to catch and lightly secure raw edges to hold flower together, as in Fig. 1-26.

11. To tack this flower to the ground fabric, pin or dab a spot of washable gluestick to hold flower in place. Place a hoop around flower to prevent the ground fabric from bunching up and distorting in size.

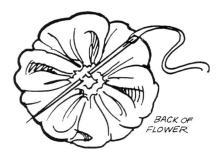

BACK OF FLOWER

Fig. 1-26

12. With a matching doubled thread, come from the back of the ground fabric up through the center of the flower. Take a small stitch, hiding it in the folds of the flower, as in Fig. 1-27.

Fig. 1-27

13. Take the next stitch about 3/8 inch away and continue securing the flower in a circular fashion moving outward and hiding stitches deep in the folds formed from the gathers. The tack stitch should draw the flower in and flatten it to the ground fabric.

The Pansy

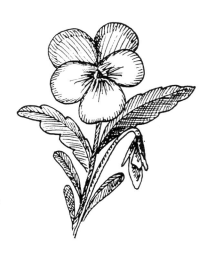

Miniature pansies can be created with silk ribbon or fabric. The petals turn out fluffier with silk ribbon.

Change color within the petals of the pansy by choos-

ing fabric or ribbon with variegated colors that swirl and change throughout.

Distinct petal color changes can be created by piecing the fabric or ribbon. Simply piece fabric or ribbon with a 1/8-inch seam allowance wherever the "u curve" begins. For example, create two purple petals and three yellow petals by piecing 2 1/8 inch of purple fabric or ribbon to 3 1/8 inch yellow fabric or ribbon. Press the seam allowance open and treat the pieced strip as one piece.

MATERIALS:

For each flower use either:

• 5 inches of 3/8-inch-wide (7 mm) silk ribbon — **or** — a straight grain strip of fabric ¾-inch wide by 5 inches long.

• The Mini Ruching Edge

• A sharp chalk marker

DIRECTIONS:

1. If using ribbon no preparation is necessary. If using fabric, fold strip in half along its length so that it is still a 5-inch-long strip and raw edges are together, right sides out.

2. Lay "u curve" edge over fabric with curved edge lying 1/8 inch up from raw edges of fabric, as shown in Fig. 1-28, or just 1/16 inch from edge of ribbon (this leaves room to mark around curve so marked lines will be near ribbon or fabric edges.

Fig. 1-28

3. Chalk around curves or pounce.

4. With a doubled regular thread, gather on "u curve" lines, as shown in Fig. 1-29, pulling gathers as you stitch to form petals. Do not knot off. Let needle dangle.

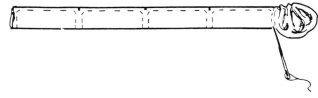

Fig. 1-29

5. Adjust gathers so first four petals are pulled tightly and the last petal is looser and wider. Gathers measure about 3/8-inch wide on last petal. Knot off.

6. Have a one-inch square of crinoline ready.

7. First, in your hand line all five petals in a row, as shown in Fig. 1-30.

Fig. 1-30

8. Lay petals 1 and 2 onto crinoline square. Using a doubled thread, take one tack stitch in the gathers of each petal to hold it to the crinoline, as shown in Fig. 1-31.

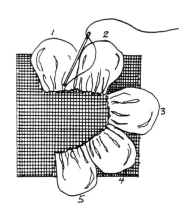

Fig. 1-31

9. Fold petals 3 and 4 to the left over the top and slightly lower than petals 1 and 2, as shown in Fig. 1-32. Take tack stitches in petal 3 and 4 in the gathers to secure.

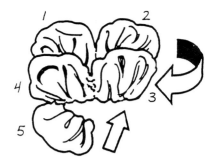

Fig. 1-32

10. Petal 5 is simply pushed upward and joins the others at the center. Tack in place, being careful to close the hole by bringing fabric and ribbon together at center.

11. Trim crinoline from pansy back so it does not show.

VARIATION: Follow steps 1 through 4. Pull the thread as tight as possible and, rather than arranging the petals as for the pansy above, form petals in one circle and tack to crinoline. Place French Knots or beads at the center.

Rosabella

This is the tiniest of my miniature flowers and it may be the easiest. This flower looks interesting clustered together in three or more flowers with a contrasting glass seed bead at its center. The flower can be made from fabric or ribbon.

MATERIALS:
• A one-inch square of fabric or ribbon in a flower color. (Use 1-inch wire ribbon and snip off the wire edges.)

• A single glass seed bead for a center, either monochromatic or contrasting

DIRECTIONS:
1. With a double thread in the needle, gather 1/8 inch in from the raw edge of the square, being careful to round the corner so that the gathering is done in one large circle inside the square, as shown in Fig. 1-33.

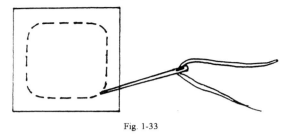

Fig. 1-33

2. Pull thread as tight as possible and knot.

3. Pull puckers outward and flatten puff.

4. Cut a ¾-inch square of crinoline. Place raw edges of puff face down centered on the crinoline.

5. With a doubled matching thread, travel from the back of the crinoline up into the center of the puff, catch seed bead and go back down into the center of the puff a few threads away to couch the bead down at center. Knot tightly to hold the bead so securely the fabric pulls inward at the center bead. Do not cut thread.

6. With a sharp chalk marker, mark four even lines from center bead dividing the puff in four equal parts, as in Fig. 1-34.

Fig. 1-34

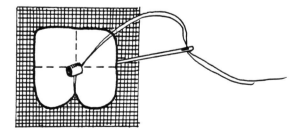

Fig. 1-35

7. With matching thread, bring thread upward under center bead, out around outside of puff encouraging thread to fall across one marked line. Needle goes back into the crinoline under the center of the puff as shown

in Fig. 1-35. Pull as tight as possible to cause fabric to dimple, and knot at back. Do not cut thread.

8. Repeat this looped stitch for remaining three lines, pulling tight and knotting after each stitch.

9. Trim crinoline away from behind Rosabella so it cannot be seen.

10. Place a hoop around quilt block before tacking Rosabella in place. Take a tack stitch at center near bead and at edges near thread.

The Sunflower

Choose golden sunflower colored fabric that is either a print of various yellow gradations or a solid yellow. Make each of the three sunflowers in the can of varying yellow colors for more realism.

DIRECTIONS:

1. For each sunflower, cut 8 circles each 1 1/8-inch in diameter, as in circle template for the daffodil in Fig. 1-7 on page 9.

Follow steps **2**, **3** and **4** for the daffodil, page 9, but make eight sunflower petals.

5. Butt raw edges of last petal and first petal together to form petals into an oval.

6. Cut a two-inch square of crinoline.

Fig. 1-36

7. Tack onto crinoline with a stick-and-stab stitch in petal folds in as small as possible oval shape, as shown in Fig. 1-36. To keep the oval small, push all petals toward center while tacking to keep inner hole as small as possible.

SUNFLOWER CENTER

Sunflower centers are ruched using The Mini Ruching Edge and can be made from either a rich brown fabric in print or solid or 7 mm silk ribbon.

1. Cut a deep brown fabric 5/8-inch wide by 7 inches long on the straight of grain or use 3/8-inch wide (7 cm) silk ribbon cut 7 inches long.

2. If using fabric, fold the fabric as if making bias tape. Since this strip is very narrow, either use a bias tape maker or try the ironing board method of making bias tape. Use spray starch to press crisply.

IRONING BOARD METHOD OF MAKING BIAS TAPE — OR — STRIPS FOR RUCHING:

Pin two straight pins to the ironing board about 12 inches apart. Make sure each pin has enough room under it to slide the width of the folded strip under exactly.

Feed the strip through the first pin with folded edges up, under the iron and then under the second pin. For fabrics that are difficult to hold a crisp crease, use a block of wood (Talon has a notion called the Clapper) to lay over the hot, pressed crease.

When cool, remove wood. Do not move the fabric until cool or the crease will not hold as well. Using spray starch on the strip before ironing keeps the tiny folds crisp.

1. Lay pressed strip with raw edges down or ribbon on sandpaper.

2. Lay the zigzag edge of The Mini Ruching Edge on top of fabric or ribbon as described in Step 3 for the Mum.

3. Using a sack of chalk like The Pouncer, slide chalk sack across the zigzag edge of The Mini Ruching Edge to mark.

NOTE: A sharp chalk marker like Clover's Chalk-O-Liner can also be used to mark The Mini Ruching Edge. However, using a sack of chalk produces a more accurate marking on the small zigzag edges.

4. Using a doubled matching thread, gather on the marked chalk line as shown in Fig. 1-20, on **Page 12**. Stitches should be about 1/8 inch long.

5. If using fabric, pull stitches as tight as possible. Once ruched, both the finished gathered fabric strip and ribbon strip should measure 2¾-inches long, not including the raw edges, as shown in Fig. 1-37.

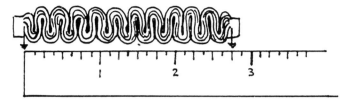

Fig. 1-37

6. Tuck and stitch raw edges of ruched strip under ends.

7. Circle ruched strip onto the top of oval sunflower petals covering raw edges of petals with ruching.

8. Using a doubled matching thread, tack ruching in place using the stick and stab stitch in the folds of the center of the ruching, as shown in Fig. 1-38.

Fig. 1-38

9. Tack the center of the ruched center together with a whip stitch or two so a hole does not form.

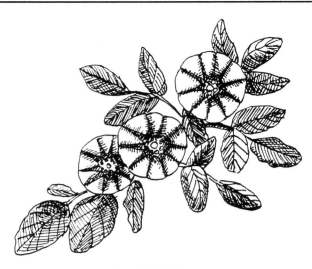

Wildflower

This wildflower is a tiny, quick-to-do flower used to fill in empty spaces or to add color into flower album blocks where needed.

MATERIALS:
Fabric 2 inches by   inch — **or** —Ribbon 3/8 inch (7mm) by 2 inches

DIRECTIONS:
1. Fold strip in half along length.

2. Gather bottom edge just about 1/16th inch up from raw edges as in Fig. 1-39. Pull gathers tight. Knot.

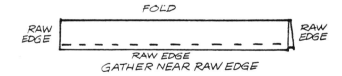

Fig. 1-39

3. Fold circle in half right sides together, matching beginning and ending sides. Seam sides with a 1/16th inch seam allowance as in Fig. 1-40.

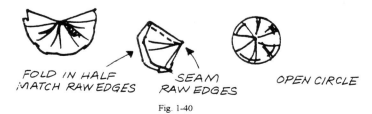

Fig. 1-40

4. Open circle.

5. Put a double strand of Balger blending filament in needle or other metallic fiber that can be threaded through a needle. When ready to appliqué wildflower to ground fabric, bring needle up through ground fabric and flower center and take a long stitch just past the outer edge of the flower into the ground fabric. Bring the needle up through the center again and continue taking long stitches just past the outer edge of the flower into the ground fabric. Continue in a wheel spoke pattern. This will add a delicate sparkle to the wildflower.

6. Stitch an iridescent bead or French knot at center.

Flower centers

This flower center can be tucked inside an old-fashioned rose, begonia, pansy or wild-flower. It is a great way to echo color by just adding a little hint of that color. It is a fun detail on album blocks.

Although this ruched center can be made from either fabric or ribbon, I prefer making it from the wired ribbon because it has a silky texture and luminescent color.

MATERIALS:
3/8-inch wide fabric strip by 1 inch cut on straight of grain — **or** — 3/8-inch wide ribbon strip by 1 inch (cut away wire edges on wired ribbon)

DIRECTIONS:
1. With a needle pull out about six threads off each edge of fabric strip starting with short ends first.

2. With a single thread in the needle, take a gathering stitch down the small island of fabric that remains at the center of the fabric strip.

3. Pull thread as tight as possible. Knot.

4. Poke this tiny, furry center inside a flower. To tack in place, come from the back of the background fabric up through the middle of the ruched center and then back down into the ruched center just a few

threads away to couch or hold the center in place. When that couching stitch is taken, the frayed edges of the ruched center should stand straight up. If they do not, make stitch tighter.

5. If the frayed, ruched center is to long for a flower, simply trim to desired length.

French Knot Center

This is a nice filling for the center of a flower. It gives the flower a very textured look.

1. The thread is brought through the fabric at the spot where the knot will be placed.

2. The thread is then held down firmly with the thumb.

3. The needle is twisted two or three times around the held thread, as in Fig. 1-41.

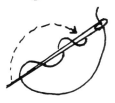

Fig. 1-41

4. With the twists still held snugly on the needle, the needle is turned and inserted back about two threads away from where the thread first emerged. As you pull the knot toward the fabric, still hold the thread snugly as it forms the knot. As in a beaded center, never make flower center in a perfect circle. Instead, create French Knots in an oval for the center.

Here is an example (Fig. 1-41A) of an oval pattern in which to bead or make French Knots. Once bead is strung on needle, go back into the fabric next to the bead, not directly under it. This allows bead to lay in proper position with side up.

Fig. 1-41A

Mad about the Leaf

Broderie Perse Leaves

It is the rich, lush colors of leaves that make flowers so attractive to look at in nature. The contrast between bright sunny flower petals against deep evergreen, olive or even kelly green leaves burnished with splashes of burgundy or plum show off a flower's colors dramatically.

Broderie Perse, a technique that was practiced about 1840 to 1850, can be used to capture leaves on today's album blocks as well. The Dictionary of Needlework 1882 edition describes this technique which was often used to make a bit of costly fabric stretch into an entire quilt:

"In broderie perse. . . applied pieces of chintz . . . representing flowers, foliage, birds and animals . . . require no backing . . . and are simply pasted on a colored foundation . . . and caught down with a stitch. . . . Stretch your background upon a frame, and paste the chintz flowers into position upon it. When the pasting is finished and dry, take the work out of the frame and stitch loosely with as little visibility as possible, all around the leaves and flowers."

Today, we can use this same technique to create lush leaves behind our 3-D flowers. The artists that design our fabrics create leaves in so many other colors than just green. It is these creatively colorful leaves that can be cut from fabric allowing a 1/8-inch seam allowance for turn under and then appliquéd onto album quilt blocks or even wearables.

To make the leaves compatible with 3-D flowers, cut a thin or low loft batting just 1/8 inch smaller than leaf shape. Appliqué about 2/3 of the way around a leaf or other shape, and then slide the batting inside the appliquéd piece. Finish appliquéing. If desired, a quilting stitch or decorative embroidery stitch can be taken down center veins on leaves for added embellishment.

RULES FOR HUNTING GREAT LEAVES FOR BRODERIE PERSE:

• Leaves need attitude. Make sure the leaves bend and bow and look like they are affected by gravity as they radiate out from the center of the design.

• Leaves should graduate in size. Select large, medium and small leaves for any design allowing the larger leaves to be closer to the center of the design with smaller leaves trailing outward.

• If appropriate, leaves can radiate in color as well as size from deepest dark to medium tones to pale. Color gradation is always pleasing to the eye.

• Not all leaves must be green. Many fabrics have green leaves splashed with pink, burgundy, eggplant or red. Use these leaves, they make the design more interesting.

• Find leaves on quilt fabric, but also tropical prints and cotton decorator prints as well.

• When appliquéing leaves in place, the needle can coax seam allowances under more in places to shape leaves. Leaves need to be shaped differently for more realism. Do not feel leaves must be perfectly shaped.

• Leaves can be cut out from fabric in groups and appliquéd in place as a group as well.

• If a fabric leaf has many tiny-ridged edges, ignore the ridges and smooth the contour of the leaf out in the appliquéing.

• Sometimes when cutting a leaf from fabric the bottom of the leaf is misshapen from other designs crossing over it. That is often okay because when tucking leaves behind flowers it is the leaf tips that will show.

• A broderie perse leaf may need a stem once appliquéd into a new design. Using the stem stitch a graceful stem can be added to the quilt block.

Quick Miniature Ribbon Leaf

Here is a very quick leaf that can be made either from French Elegance wire ribbon or fabric. This leaf is great tucked behind flowers singly or in groups.

MATERIALS:
1¼ inch of French Elegance wire ribbon 5/8 inch wide— or — 1¼-inch square of cotton or lightweight silk fabric

DIRECTIONS:
1. For each leaf, cut a piece of ribbon 1¼-inches long or fabric 1¼-inches square.

2. If using fabric, fold square in half. The following directions apply to both fabric and ribbon. Fold fabric or ribbon in half like a book with right sides out as in Fig. 2-1 to mark the half with a crease.

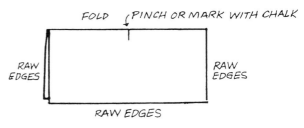

Fig 2-1

3. Fold top right corner down along center fold. Fold top left corner down along center fold so that a point is formed as in Fig.2-2.

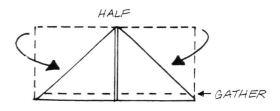

Fig. 2-2

4. Gather across long edge catching all layers. Pull as tight as possible and knot off. Either the plain side of the leaf or the side of the leaf with the ribbon edges centered can be used.

Templates for leaves

1. Trace leaf shape onto quilter's template plastic labeling each template with all information printed on the leaf pattern including grain lines if applicable.

2. Cut leaf from plastic on pencil line.

3. On a piece of sandpaper or sandpaper board, lay leaf template on **right** side of fabric and trace around the leaf shape with a pencil.

4. Next, cut out the leaf shape from fabric adding a 1/8-inch seam allowance while cutting. (Just estimate the size of the seam allowance while cutting.)

5. Store labeled leaf templates in a zip lock bag.

The Album Blocks

Fig. 3-1

Friendship's Bond

This block is a great way to spotlight a favorite fabric. Choose a fabric with good contrast to the background block. If choosing a print, try cutting all four hearts from the exact same position on the print.

The block can be made with plain, stuffed hearts or with flowers and leaves grouped on each heart. If embellishing the hearts with flowers, be careful to choose a less-busy fabric that will allow the flowers to show off.

MATERIALS:

• 6½-inch background block

• About 8-inch square of print fabric for hearts

• Optional for flowers: either four, 9-inch-long pieces of 7 mm silk ribbon — **or** — four, ¾-inch wide by 9-inch long strips of flower-colored fabric — **or** — four, ¾-inch wide by 9-inch long strips of Artemis bias silk ribbon

• Eight, 1¼-inch by 5/8-inch French wire ribbon pieces for leaves — **or** — eight, 2-inch squares of green fabric for leaves

• About 8-inch square thin batting

• A working board

DIRECTIONS:

1. Cut a background fabric 6½ inches square on grain.

2. Fold and press square in half and in half again to mark the block into four equal parts as in Fig. 3-2.

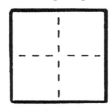

Fig. 3-2

The four hearts can be laid out two different ways on the block. Choose the one you prefer. In Friendship's Bond in The Garden Sampler (see color photo), the points of the hearts point out toward the center of each side. In The Enchanted Garden (see color photo), the heart points are pointing toward each corner of the block.

The template placement guide shows the layout for Friendship's Bond in The Garden Sampler.

When laying out the hearts for The Enchanted Garden, lay four hearts roughly in place. Arrange the hearts so that the pencil appliqué lines of each heart butt up against the adjoining heart. Heart points should point squarely toward each corner of the block. (My heart points were 1¾ inch from raw edge corners, although the distance may vary based on pencil lines.)

CHOOSE EITHER:

Method A: Traditional Appliqué and padded hearts — **or** — **Method B**: Reverse Appliqué with no padding

A. TRADITIONAL APPLIQUE:
(The easier and more dimensional of the two methods)

3. Before appliquéing the final side of each heart in place, lay a thin layer of batting inside each heart to pad. Finish appliquéing.

B. REVERSE APPLIQUE:

Important: Follow these steps in order for success.

3. Trace all four hearts onto a 6-inch square of template plastic.

4. Only cut out the heart shape of two opposite hearts making sure that your cutting line is just outside your pencil line. So you have a window template, as in Fig. 3-3.

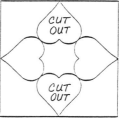

Fig. 3-3

5. Trace all four hearts onto background fabric marking first two hearts around heart windows. Next, turn the template one-quarter turn, lining up heart lines and mark the remaining two hearts through the window.

6. Cut out inside of hearts leaving a 3/16-inch seam allowance from pencil line toward center of each heart. You are cutting out the inside of each heart but leaving a seam allowance to turn under.

7. Cut out a 6½-inch square of fabric to fill heart shapes.

8. Pin or glue baste (using water-soluble glue) top cut out fabric on top of bottom heart fabric.

9. Reverse appliqué hearts in place.

A. First, fingerpress raw inside edges of hearts under.

B. Appliqué opposite hearts first. Then appliqué the connecting hearts between.

Note: When seam allowance shows tension horizontally, clip curves to within 2 threads of seam line.

10. Trim excess bottom fabric layer away to within ¼-inch seam allowance around hearts.

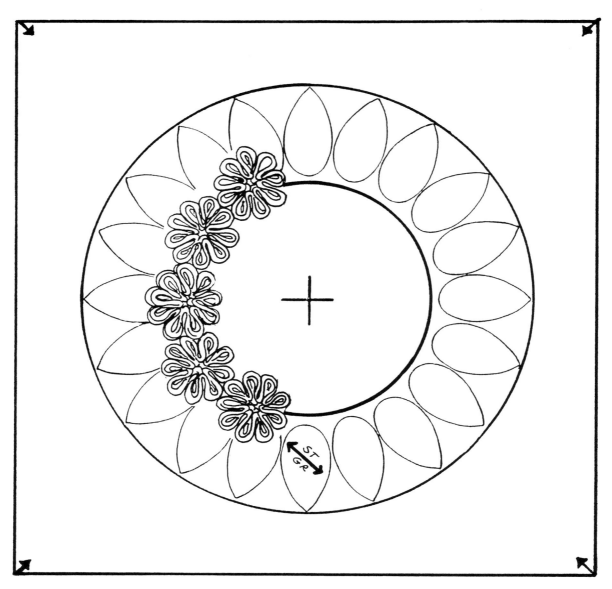

Fig. 3-4

This placement guide shows a partial view of the ruched mums that cover the leaf bottoms. In finished block, ruched mums make a complete circle around leaves as in color photo of Encircling Peace.

Encircling Peace

This is a simple wreath of 12 ruched miniature flowers and 20 almond-shaped leaves. The flowers can be made from 7 mm silk ribbon or fabric.

The secret to being accomplished at appliqué is to practice it. Appliqué is a learned skill that requires practice. This wreath will do just that for you. As you appliqué each leaf in this wreath, you should feel your appliqué skills improving, and by the time your reach the 20th leaf, you should be a pro.

MATERIALS:
- 6½-inch square background fabric on grain

- Twelve 5-inch pieces of 7 mm variegated silk ribbon in one flower color — **or** — twelve 5-inch long pieces of 7 mm silk ribbon in different flower colors

- 1/8 yard of leaf-printed fabric so that the leaf vein or pattern from the printed leaves can be centered on a 1-inch long by ½-inch wide leaf shape

- Sharp chalk marker

- The Mini Ruching Edge

- Five-inch embroidery hoop

- A working board

DIRECTIONS:
1. Cut a background fabric 6½ inches square on grain.

2. Fold and press square in half and in half again to mark the block into four equal parts.

3. Trace one leaf shape onto see-through plastic for leaf template.

ABOUT LEAF FABRIC:
Your 100 percent cotton leaf fabric may be any of these three types:

- covered with actual different leaves larger than leaf shape;

- one solid color green;

- variegated green shades.

4. Trace 20 leaves from fabric either capturing a center leaf vein in the center of the leaf template shape (Fig. 3-5) or capturing other leaf colors or designs in each shape. Add a 3/16-inch seam allowance around each leaf when cutting leaves from fabric.

Fig. 3-5

5. Fingerpress seam allowance under on all 20 leaves or prepare using your favorite method of appliqué.

6. Place background fabric block over Figure 3-4 as a guide that can be seen through the fabric to determine leaf placement.

NOTE: If background block fabric is not see through, make a photo copy of Fig. 3-4, cut out leaf tips in one whole piece and transfer outline of leaves to fabric with chalk marker.

Lay leaves on background block so that individual leaf tips are just touching outer circle. With a pencil lightly mark wider leaf bottoms that form the inner circle. (These lines will be covered with ruched silk flowers and will not show.) With ¾-inch appliqué pins, pin leaves in place using pencil lines as a guide. Appliqué leaves in place.

ADDING THE FLOWERS
7. Position flowers atop bottom of leaves at the compass points: north, south, east and west.

8. Next position two flowers between each of the first four flowers.

9. Using quilter's straight pins, pin each mini flower in place carefully. Arrange mini mums so that the widest part of each flower touches the next flower and the scalloped petals of each flower fit between the petals of the next flower like a jigsaw puzzle around the circle.

10. Make sure the flowers form a nice round circle. When satisfied with positions, place a dab of washable gluestick behind each flower. Poke a pin to hold each flower in place until glue dries.

11. Place a five-inch embroidery hoop around entire ring of flowers and leaves.

12. Using a double thread and milliner's needle, tack flower petals to fabric sticking and stabbing tack stitch in tiny folds of petals.

NOTE: When tacking flowers in place, take time to spread petals of each flower and manipulate silk ribbon to make flower full and pretty.

Fig. 3-6

Petals & Ribbons

This wreath and its leaves and flowers are made solely from French Elegance wire ribbon. The ribbon behaves like fabric. It is colorfast without prewashing. It launders beautifully as long as the ribbon is secured to the background. A few areas - like the bow, for instance — can be left freestanding as long as the greater portion of ribbon bow is appliquéd in place.

While this ribbon was used to opulently wrap boxes of chocolate and other gifts in France, quilters have become quite enamored with it because of the magnificent range of color gradation each ribbon affords.

MATERIALS:

- 6½ inch square background fabric.
- 1 yard French Elegance wire ribbon 5/8 inch wide in a graduated shades of midnight blue
- Five pieces of 5/8-inch-wide French Elegance wire ribbon flower color each 7 inches long
- Five pieces of 5/8-inch-wide French Elegance wire ribbon soft yellow each 1¼ inches long
- Long quilter's pins with glass heads
- 6-inch long ruler
- A working board

FIRST MAKE THE WREATH:

1. Cut a background fabric 6½ inches square on grain.

2. Fold and press square in half and in half again to mark the block in four equal parts. Spread block on working board.

3. Fold 1 yard of midnight blue ribbon in half and open leaving a crease to mark the center 15 inches in from either edge.

4. Lay center fold of ribbon roughly an inch from the top of block. Poke a pin at the center fold straight into the board holding the ribbon in place.

NOTE: In creating the ribbon wreath, all pins will be poked straight into the board so pins are standing up.

5. Taking raw edges of ribbon in hands, cross ribbon and tie until the ribbon forms a circle. When both tails measure 8 inches long each from the loose tie, stop and poke a pin at lose tie.

6. Begin to fold and crease ribbon circle irregularly forming it into a smaller circle. Poke pin in place.

NOTE: The wreath should lie about 1 inch from the raw edge of the 6½-inch square background block at its widest points. So work with the six-inch ruler, continually measuring the distance the wreath is from the raw edge of the block as the wreath is formed.

6. Tie the bow. Tails should be about 5 inches long each from the bow knot.

7. Fluff and position the bow and tighten the knot until you like the look of it. Poke pin in place.

8. Fold the tails back and forth and upward so tails follow the contour of the wreath. Take your time and play with the entire shape of the wreath, shape of the bows and tails to form a round design.

9. Unpin wreath once you like the folds and creases and reposition the wreath so that it is centered on the background block. Poke pins to hold wreath in place. The wire in the ribbon will allow the crinkled ribbon to hold its shape even though unpinned.

10. Using a popsicle stick or toothpick and a washout gluestick, remove each pin carefully and slide a bit of glue under the ribbon wreath to temporarily tack it in place before appliqué. Place each pin back to hold the glue securely until it dries.

11. Appliqué the edges of the ribbon in place just like fabric. The ribbon wreath can be appliquéd in place anywhere the edge or fold of the ribbon is touching the background block. It is very easy to hide appliqué stitches in the woven edge of the ribbon that covers the wire.

12. Tack each loop of the bow down on three sides allowing one side to remain dimensional.

13. Create 5 hepatica to position on wreath. See flowers, page 10.

14. Create 10 quick leaves to place behind hepatica on wreath. See Leaves, page 20.

APPLIQUE FLOWERS IN PLACE:

1. Arrange five flowers evenly spaced on top of the wreath circle. Poke pin in place on working board.

2. Arrange two quick miniature leaves behind each flower. Poke pin in place.

3. Using a popsicle stick or toothpick with washout gluestick, remove pins that hold leaves and slide a bit of glue behind each leaf to temporarily hold it in place. Place a bit more glue on top of leaf where flower will sit and press flower in place. Place pins back through leaves and flowers to hold glue securely until it dries.

4. To tack leaves in place, use a doubled matching thread and take tiny stick and stab stitches down the center of each leaf. Take additional tack stitches in gathers. Knot off behind each leaf before tacking the next.

5. Next, tack flowers in place hiding tack stitches in scalloped petals of flowers.

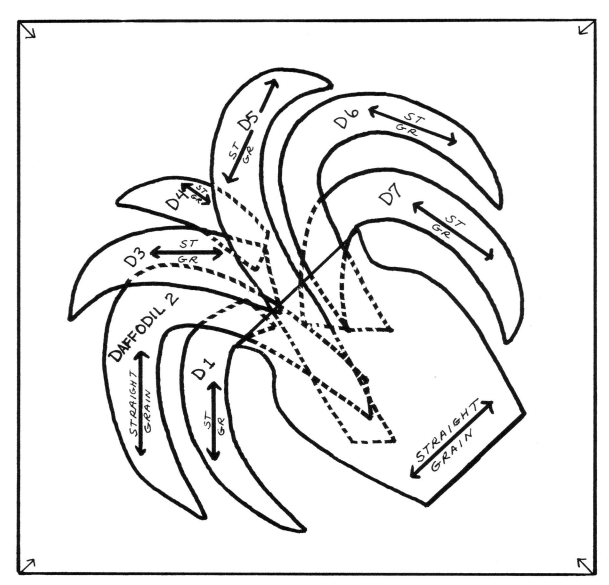

Fig. 3-7

Daffodil Splendor

Choose a dark mottled, swirled, marbled or even cracked print that can capture the random character of art glass for this vase and which will contrast richly with the background fabric. The shape of this vase is designed to be easy to appliqué and yet show a fine silhouette in a quilt block as leaves surround it. For the leaves, choose deep greens that show off lovely yellow daffodils of varying tones of yellow and cream.

The Enchanted Garden

Spring's Blessing

Love Is . . .

Elegant Bounty

Sunshine's Joy

Encircling Peace

Daffodil Splendor

Friendship's Bond

Welcoming Begonias

Petals & Ribbons

The Garden Sampler

MATERIALS:

• 6½-inch square background fabric on grain

• 25 circles, each one 1 1/8 inches in diameter cut from various tones of yellow for petals

• Five, 5-inch by 3/8 inch (7 mm) pieces of silk ribbon — **or** — five, 5-inch by 5/8-inch wide pieces of fabric for daffodil centers

out a 6-inch square of a mottled fabric for vase

‑ Seven different monochromatic green prints for leaves

• A 6-inch square of thin batting for behind leaves

• A working board

DIRECTIONS:

1. Cut a background block 6½-inches square on grain.

2. Fold and press square in half and in half again to mark the block into four equal parts.

3. Appliqué sides and bottom of vase onto block following template placement guide (Fig. 3-7). Leave top vase edge open.

4. Choose a variety of green print fabrics. Each of the seven leaves could be a different print. It is important to choose a green fabric that flower colors will show up dramatically on and green fabric that shows up richly against background block. Appliqué leaves in place as in template placement guide (Fig. 3-7) or to your own arrangement.

5. Make daffodil petals and centers for five daffodils. See flowers, page 9.

6. Arrange five daffodils on top of leaves and vase to your liking or follow placement guide. Tack in place.

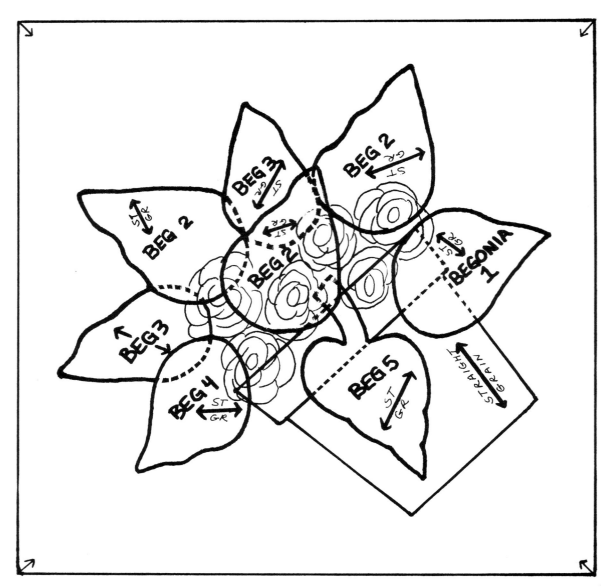

Fig. 3-8

Welcoming Begonias

This is a classic clay pot from the gardening shed that can be filled with whatever you like. Choose many tones and shades of rich green to create the asymmetrical tuberous begonia leaf — a leaf that is truly a work of art from nature.

The begonia is a profuse flower of many magical glowing and stunning two-color combinations. Finding fabric to capture the beguiling colors of begonias is a challenge. I have long searched for the perfect shaded fabric for tuberous begonias — a champagne pink that fades into magenta would be perfect.

Here is a list of possible begonia colors to inspire your fabric selections: salmon tinged with soft pink; pink flushed white; vivid orange; bright crimson; coral red; white flecked with pink; pale pink with darker pink spots; green to white; pink with red; cream white; rose-pink; pale rose; orange-apricot; ʳlet; canary yellow; soft apricot; orange ₍ₗₗₒw; and white with crinkled red edges.

Search for these two-color blends that melt into each other and glow ever so grandly against deep green asymmetrical leaves.

DIRECTIONS:

1 Cut a background block 6½ inches square on grain.

2. Fold and press square in half and in half again to mark the block into four equal parts.

3. Center clay pot so top edge of pot top lies along center line.

4. Both pieces of clay pot will have batting underneath. Appliqué clay pot top down first leaving the bottom edge open so that the clay pot bottom can slide under. Slide a layer of batting cut 1/8 inch smaller than template behind the clay pot top.

5. Appliqué clay pot bottom. Before appliquéing final side of pot bottom in place slide a layer of batting cut 1/8 inch smaller than template behind the pot bottom. Finish appliquéing pot in place.

6. Cut out seven begonia leaves and arrange as in photograph or in your own arrangement. Add additional leaves if needed to fill arrangement. Appliqué about 2/3 of each leaf in place then slide a layer of batting behind leaf and finish appliquéing.

7. Make 2 large 12-petal Begonias and four or five, 9-petal Begonias to fill clay pot to your liking. See Old-Fashioned Rose or Begonia instructions, page 12-14.

8. Pin flowers in place on fabric. Place hoop around flowers. Tack begonias in place with a stick and stab stitch between the folds of each flower.

Fig. 3-9

Sunshine's Joy

This is a simple appliquéd watering can filled with three-dimensional sunflowers. The leaves and watering can are appliquéd and stuffed with a layer of batting behind each.

Stringing all the 3-D petals on one thread as each flower is produced makes this block faster, easier and pleasant to sew.

MATERIALS:

• 24 circles each 1 1/8-inch in diameter cut from various golden sunflower gradations

• Three, brown fabric strips 5/8-inch wide by 7 inches on straight grain — **or** — Three brown 7 mm silk ribbon pieces each 7 inches long

• The Mini Ruching Edge

   sharp chalk

• An 8-inch square of mottled gray fabric for watering can

• 1/8 yard of green leaf fabric for a bias strip cut 7/8 - inch wide by 8 inches

• Five leaves to broderie perse or green fabric to use with templates

• Thin batting to lay under watering can and leaves

DIRECTIONS:

1. Cut a background fabric 6½ inches square on grain.

2. Fold and press square in half and in half again to mark the block into four equal parts.

3. Make sunflower petals and centers for three sunflowers. See Flowers, page 17.

MAKE 3/16-INCH WIDE BIAS STEMS:

1. Cut a strip of stem-colored fabric on the true bias 8 inches long by 7/8 inch wide.

2. Fold strip in half along length with wrong sides together and press.

3. With a thread that does not match, machine stitch 3/16 inch from the raw edge of folded strip as in Fig. 3-10.

FOLD

MACHINE SEW BIAS STRIP TOGETHER FIRST.

Fig. 3-10

4. Transfer just one thin pencil line to background block where bias stems are to lie. Follow template placement guide (Fig. 3-7).

5. Cut bias strip into three small pieces to cover stem lines as in Fig. 3-11.

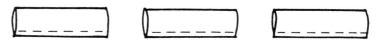

Fig. 3-11

6. Lay bias stem pieces on lines so that machine stitching covers pencil line. (The raw edge of pieces should lie on the smaller curve while the fold lies on the larger curve as in Fig. 3-12.

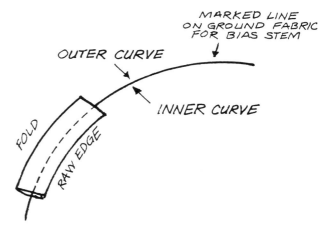

MARKED LINE ON GROUND FABRIC FOR BIAS STEM

OUTER CURVE

INNER CURVE

FOLD

RAW EDGE

Fig. 3-12

7. Pin in place being careful to place pins parallel to stem so that you can withdraw them as you machine sew toward them.

8. Machine sew with matching thread just outside first stitching (between first stitching and fold) all the way to the end of each bias piece as in Fig. 3-13.

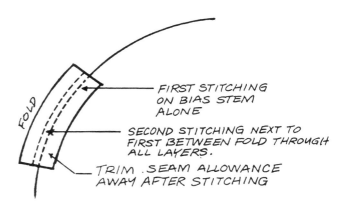

FOLD

FIRST STITCHING ON BIAS STEM ALONE

SECOND STITCHING NEXT TO FIRST BETWEEN FOLD THROUGH ALL LAYERS.

TRIM SEAM ALLOWANCE AWAY AFTER STITCHING

Fig. 3-13

9. Trim seam allowance away.

10. Press bias stem over stitching toward small curve as in Fig. 3-14.

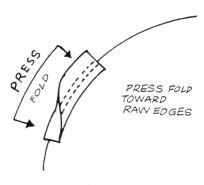

Fig. 3-14

11. Hand appliqué remaining side of bias stem in place.

APPLIQUEING THE WATERING CAN:

1. When cutting out the pieces of the watering can, pay close attention to straight of grain lines. Laying the straight of grain lines down so that they run parallel to the straight lines of the body of the can and parallel to the spout of the can will make the design easy to appliqué. Watch the grain line on the handle as well. This insures that the bias lies on the curve of the handle, which insures easy and beautiful appliqué.

2. Cut each piece out adding just a 1/8-inch seam allowance on all sides.

3. Appliqué pieces in place using your favorite method of appliqué.

4. When appliquéing a larger piece like the body of the watering can, use a dab of washout glue stick to hold the piece in position as well as pinning it every couple of inches. Sometimes larger pieces tend to move out of position more easily. Using a dab of glue stick on all appliqué pieces is a great way to insure each piece stays in position during the stitching.

5. The watering can and leaves will all be made more dimensional by adding a layer of batting behind each. Cut the batting about 1/8 inch smaller than the actual piece on all sides. With larger pieces like the watering can and spout, appliqué two sides down and leave one side open to slide the batting in. Then finish appliquéing the piece. Appliqué one side of leaf in place and around the leaf tip and then lay batting in.

ORDER OF FINISHING THE BLOCK:

1. Appliqué bias stems in place.

2. Appliqué watering can in place.

3. Tack Sunflowers in place.

4. Appliqué leaves in place.

Fig. 3-15

Love Is ...

This quilt block set inside a heart shape idealizes the vision of the loving parent nurturing the nest. The three-dimensional bird's nest is easy and fun to make and gives the feel and texture of fur. The nest is washable and will not fray any further than intended.

The bird can be constructed of one piece or more. The background of the heart can be a pale sky landscape to give a quiet setting to the scene.

MATERIALS:

• 6½ inch square background block on grain

• Bias strip 7/8-inch wide by 25 inches in a shade deeper than background fabric to trim heart

• 5¼-inch square of fabric for behind bird and scene in pale color (see step 5)

• 3-inch square fabric for bird and other colors to piece bird if preferred

• 12 leaves cut from leaf fabric —or — green fabric to cut leaves from templates

• 5-inch square taupe- or gray-colored fabric or other color for branch

• Seven different brown or green fabrics, 3 inch by 1½-inch wide (some medium, some dark)

• Small pieces of pale blue fabric for eggs

• Thin batting for behind all pieces

• Green embroidery floss

• Pigma Pen for marking bird

• Optional: bead for bird's eye

DIRECTIONS:

1. Cut a background fabric 6½ inches square on grain.

2. Fold and press square in half and in half again to mark the block into four equal parts.

3. The line outlining the heart is thick. Trace around the outside of that line onto 6½-inch square block.

4. Cut out heart on this line.

5. Place 5¼-inch square background fabric behind heart opening making sure to allow fabric to cover opening with at least ½-inch of fabric around all sides. (Choose a light fabric that coordinates especially with background fabric i.e. sky blue, pink, pale green something with a bit of pale color or even a true sky like fabric for a landscape look).

6. Glue stick right side of heart just on outer ¼-inch edge of square to wrong side of background block.

7. Cut one branch from a taupe mottled or solid fabric adding a 1/8-inch seam allowance on all sides when cutting.

8. Cut one nest center adding 1/8-inch seam allowance on all sides.

9. Cut 7 nest pieces, being careful to follow grain lines in various shades of brown or dark green or a mix of both colors and add 1/8-inch seam allowance on all sides.

10. Layer all 7 nest pieces right sides up. Choose a shade on bottom that will contrast nicely with top fabric. (Both top and bottom fabrics will show the most).

11. With a sharp chalk marker, draw straight lines in rows 3/16 inch apart that lie on the true bias as in Fig. 3-16. Machine sew with a shorter length stitch (2 mm) on lines, remembering to back tack at the beginning and end of each line of stitching.

Fig 3-16

12. Using a sharp small scissors, slice through the *top six layers of fabric* between all machine stitched rows.

13. Wet nest and wash with soap lathering it up and rubbing the fabric against itself abrasively to encourage fraying. Rinse. Dry in the dryer if possible or in an airtight plastic bag with a hair dryer in class.

14. Appliqué branch down first — no need to appliqué top branch edge where nest will sit between lines on branch template. Appliqué top edge of branch first, then lay a thin layer of batting under it. (Trim batting 1/8 inch on all sides to fit under piece). Pin. Finish appliquéing branch. Trim shape of nest with scissors if necessary.

15. Pin or baste (or glue stick) nest center in place. Appliqué top edge of nest center only.

16. Pin the frayed nest in place. *Machine sew only sides of nest in place,* by sewing right down the slashed fabric on both edges of the nest. Remember to back tack at beginning and end of stitching. (The rest of the nest will be sewed down after the eggs are

tucked inside).

17. Tuck 1, 2 or 3 eggs in nest. Make each egg a different tone of pale blue or pale green if you have done a Robin or Bluebird. (If you piece a different bird, check a bird book and match egg color). Appliqué half of egg. Lay a bit of batting inside egg. Finish appliqué.

Egg Template

18. Finish tacking frayed nest in place by machine sewing down slashed channels of nest. (Stitches will be hidden in channels.)

19. Optional: Collect about one teaspoon of loose threads from nest fabric and lay on top of nest. Using a matching thread, couch loose threads to nest surface.

20. Cut out Mountain Bluebird in either one complete piece or with contrasting chest. Do not appliqué tail down yet. Appliqué half of bird, lay thin batting inside and then finish appliqué. Leave ¾-inch of tail unappliquéd where tail laps over heart edge.

21. This piping is easy. One of the biggest worries with piping is beginning and ending. In this heart, the beginning and ending raw edges are hidden under the bird's tail. Follow these simple steps and the piping fits together onto the heart just like a jigsaw puzzle.

A. Choose a color fabric in a deeper shade of background to pipe around heart.

B. Cut a strip on true bias 7/8 inch x 25 inches

C. Fold strip in half with wrong sides together. Press.

D. On this strip only, machine sew 3/16 inch from raw edge.

E. Lay raw edge of bias strip on raw edge of heart (with fold outside heart.) Pin in place keeping raw edge of strip even with raw edge of heart.

F. Beginning and ending at point where bird's tail will cover piping, machine sew just inside first stitching between first stitching and fold around heart. (By simply sewing inside first stitching it is easy to machine sew smoothly around heart.)

G. Trim raw edge from bias close to stitching so when fold is pressed toward center it will cover raw edge. (Be careful not to cut heart fabric.)

H. Press fold over stitching.

22. Appliqué remaining side of bias trim in place.

23. Appliqué bird's tail over beginning and end tails of bias.

24. Pen in details on bird with .05 Pigma Pen if desired. Embroider an eye with a French Knot (page 19) or sew a tiny black bead in for eye.

25. Cut 12 or more leaves from a leaf fabric and arrange and appliqué in place around bird. Place a layer of thin batting behind each leaf before completely appliquéing leaf in place.

26. Using the stem stitch, embroider a stalk for leaves using two strands of embroidery floss.

STEM STITCH: This is an adapted stem stitch that allows this stitch to follow any drawn line smoothly and evenly without ridges that sometimes typify traditional stem stitch. The trick is that each stitch is "scoop stitched" into the hole of the last stitch. This stitch is wonderful for quickly filling in stems of leaves, winding vines and very effective for signing your name, initials or date.

To begin, draw a graceful stem and bring the thread up at "A" at the start of the stem. Staying on the line, scoop into the fabric "B" about ¼ inch away from "A" and come up between the two stitches at "C" as in Fig. 3-17. Always keep the thread lying to the right or the left, whichever preferred.

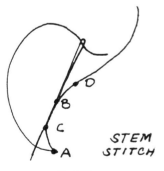

Fig 3-17

Scoop into the fabric again at "D" emerging at "B." Continue. To end, always go into the fabric one final time maintaining the slant of the stitch. Always work the stitch about 1/8 inch [3 mm] and work the stitch closer together on curves.

27. To finish off block, trim the excess fabric from square (heart inset) on back of background block to within ¼ inch of machine stitching around heart.

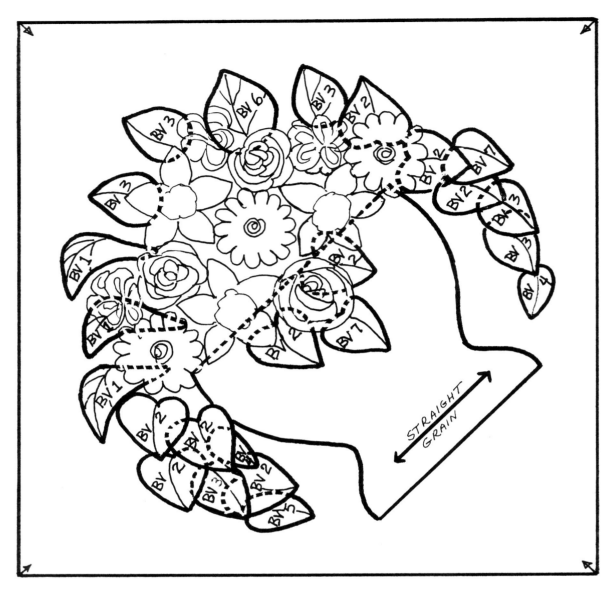

Fig. 3-18

Elegant Bounty

This is a multi-color bouquet in a simple-shaped vase that is easy to stitch. Graceful curves and a great silhouette make this vase eye-catching. Create it from a deep dark fabric either in a solid or a print that reads like a solid. Make sure the vase fabric contrasts strongly with the background fabric. In the model pictured, the back of a fabric was used to give the vase a quiet elegance.

Four different dimensional flowers — the daffodil, the pansy, the hepatica and the old-fashioned rose — mingle texture and color to fill the vase.

MATERIALS:

- 6½-inch background block on grain

- Three, 7-inch by 5/8 inch wide French Elegance ribbon in a flower color

- Three, 1¼-inch by 5/8 inch wide French Elegance ribbon in yellow for flower centers

- Fifteen, 1 1/8 inch in diameter circles cut from daffodil colored fabric for petals

- Three, 5-inch strips of 7 mm silk ribbon for daffodil centers — or — three, 5-inch strips of fabric by 5/8-inch wide for daffodil centers

- Three, 5-inch strips of 7 mm silk ribbon for pansies — or — three, 5-inch strips of fabric by 5/8-inch wide for pansies

- Three, 9-inch strips by ¾-inches wide either fabric — or — Artemis silk ribbon for peonies

- About 20 to 25 leaves cut from a fabric printed with leaves to broderie perse — or — cut 20 to 25 leaves from a green solid or print fabric using heart leaf templates.

DIRECTIONS:

1. Cut a background block 6½ inches square on grain.

2. Fold and press square in half and in half again to mark the block into four equal parts.

3. Center vase on block with vase top edge along center line. Dab some washout glue stick under vase to hold piece in place. Pin piece every inch or so to prevent the piece from slipping or moving as you sew.

4. Appliqué vase on sides and bottom. Leave top edge open. Before appliquéing last side slide a thin layer of batting behind and then finish appliquéing vase in place.

LEAVES FOR THE ELEGANT VASE:

1. For miniature quilt blocks, like the 6-inch block, seek fabrics that have smaller leaf shapes that are about ¾-inch square. Cut out about 20 leaves or more if necessary that will drip down the sides of the vase and also frame all the flowers at the center. If preferred, cut 20 or more leaves from a green solid or print fabric using heart leaf templates.

2. Once the background block with vase appliquéd is completed, lay the block on a small working board.

3. Tentatively arrange leaves around vase and poke pins straight into the board to hold leaves temporarily in position.

MAKE A BOUQUET OF FLOWERS:

Make all the flowers first for this vase and then arrange then to your liking before appliquéing leaves and flowers in place.

1. Make three miniature pansies. See pages 14-16.

2. Make three miniature Hepatica. See pages 10-11.

3. Make three miniature daffodils. See pages 9-10.

4. Make three miniature old-fashioned roses, see pages 12-14.

5. On working board, arrange flowers atop leaves. (Leaves should not be appliquéd in place as yet so that you can continue to arrange leaves and flowers.) When satisfied with arrangement, dab of bit of washout glue stick behind leaves.

6. Move flowers off leaves temporarily. Appliqué leaves in place. Remember to slide a thin layer of batting behind leaves before appliquéing the final side of each leaf in place.

7. Once leaves are appliquéd, dab of bit of washout glue stick behind flowers and place in position. To tack all flowers in place, place a hoop around background fabric where flower will be stitched. Tack using a doubled thread, as in Fig. 3-19.

Fig 3-19

Fig. 3-20

Spring's Blessing

(An exercise in color choice)

"Spring's Blessing" is a very easy basket to appliqué and shows off the show-stopping twisted basket handle. Fill the basket with all pansies or a mixed bouquet of flowers.

What makes this basket so delightful is that the quilter becomes the florist. In this role, the quilter can bring together color and flowers by following a simple step-by-step evolution of playing with color. Take these simple steps with me one by one and watch how color comes to life right before your eyes. What you will see is how complementary color combinations will *guide you and help you develop a stronger sense of color. Follow the dialogue in italic type between the construction steps, and together we will explore color without a lot of hard-to-understand technical terms.*

You don't have to choose all your colors right away. Start by picking a background fabric and a basket bottom fabric. For the basket, choose a less busy fabric, a print that reads like a solid or a solid. The basket is like the plain canvas that will have a riot of color (and flowers) on top of it.

CHOOSE YOUR COLORS:

In choosing basket and background, make one choice: Decide between warm tones or cool tones.

Warm tones are colors dominated by yellow in their mixing. Consider whether you like warm tones like yellow, yellow greens, orange and red. If so, choose a warm-colored basket like a mustard or tawny brown and choose a warmer-toned background fabric as well.

Cool tones are dominated by blue in their mixing. Do you prefer cool tones like blue violet, fuschia, cherry red and blue green? Choose a white background or a cool tone background like pale pink, pale blue or a swirling mixture.

A simple color exercise that is easy to do anywhere at anytime is to look closely at things in your daily life. Try to classify the color you see by "warm" or "cool." If you are driving down the highway admiring the trees, look closer. Notice if the trees are a yellow green and warm tones, or if they are in the shade and more blue green and cool tones.

MATERIALS:
- 6½-inch square on grain background fabric

- 2/3 yard of overdyed French wire ribbon, preferably 5/8-inch wide but 1-inch-wide wire ribbon will do

- A 3-inch by 5-inch square of cotton fabric for basket bottom to match ribbon

- Wash-out fabric gluestick

- Popsicle stick, toothpick or wood skewer

- Long quilter's straight pins with heads

- A 7-inch square working board

- 9 pieces of 5-inch long 7 mm silk ribbon for miniature pansies

- The Mini Ruching Edge

- Sharp chalk marker

DIRECTIONS:

1. Cut a background fabric 6½ inches square on grain.

2. Fold and press square in half and in half again to mark the block into four equal parts.

3. Make a plastic template for the basket bottom tracing the actual size from Fig. 3-20 onto see-through plastic.

4. Trace around basket bottom template onto fabric. When cutting the basket from fabric add a 3/16-inch seam allowance at the sides and bottom of the basket only.

5. Fold basket in half vertically to find center.

6. Lay basket on background fabric so top edge of basket lies on center fold horizontally and center fold of basket lies on vertical fold on background block as in Fig. 3-21.

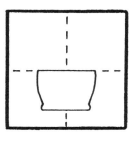

Fig 3-21

7. Carefully pin basket bottom in place very well using ¾-inch appliqué or pleating pins, or dab some washable glue stick in just a few spots to hold basket in place so it will not slide out of position when sewing around it.

8. Appliqué sides and bottom of basket in place.

Miniature Twisted Basket Handle

BUILD COLORS:

Overdyed French wire ribbon comes in a variety of multi-colored combinations. But if you look closely at the ribbon, you will see an overdyed ribbon that is predominately warm colors and another overdyed ribbon that is predominately cool colors.

Based on your first color decision, choose a warm or cool ribbon for the basket handle that coordinates with your basket. If you are unsure, "audition" the ribbons. Have nothing more than the background block and appliquéd basket bottom on top of your working board. Move all other colored fabric or other color distractions away. It is important that when you audition color, you only audition one color choice at a time because colors bounce off each other. It is that bouncing that we are looking for.

Lay the warm colored ribbon next to your basket. Take it away and then try the cool colored ribbon. The color answer should be obvious. The colors should brighten and heighten. We're not looking for an exact match here. What we're looking for is colors that say "yes" emphatically to you. If you are still unsure, just go with what looks best to you. Guess what, that's the correct color.

DIRECTIONS:

9. A working board is very important in making this block.

    A. Cut a 7-inch square of corrugated cardboard. The cardboard must be corrugated — two layers of cardboard with waffle grooves and air sandwiched in between.

    B. Totally cover the surface of the board with batting or felt and glue in place. Fabric pieces will stick nicely to this surface.

10. Lay out background block with appliquéd basket bottom on working board.

11. Slide "Miniature Twisted Basket Handle Guide" behind quilt block lining up the basket bottom as in

Fig. 3-22. Make sure background block lies flat. Poke a couple of pins straight into the board to hold the paper and fabric in place.

Miniature Twisted Basket "Handle Guide"

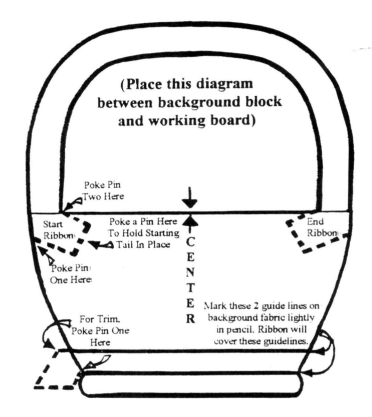

Fig. 3-22

12. Prepare the overdyed French wire ribbon: (Overdyed ribbon is strongly recommended because of the wonderful range of colors in the ribbon. It is like a rainbow and when the rainbow is twisted and folded back and forth on itself, it makes a spectacular handle.)

    A. For this miniature basket handle, 24 inches of 5/8-inch wide French overdyed wire ribbon is used. (If 1-inch wide ribbon is used, the method that follows is the same, simply fold the wider ribbon in thirds along its length rather than in half.)

    B. Find the wrong side of ribbon. (Many times, the colors are not as dramatic on the wrong side of the ribbon. The edge that is woven over the wire lies flat and sometimes looks whiter on the wrong side.) Coat the wrong side of the ribbon completely with wash-out

C. If using the 5/8-inch wide ribbon, fold the ribbon in half along its length allowing the woven edges that cover the wires to lie next to each other as in Fig. 3-23.

Fold 5/8-inch wide ribbon in half along the length

Fig 3-23

If using the 1-inch wide ribbon, first fold the ribbon 1/3 of the way in, as in Fig. 3-24.

Fold 1-inch wide ribbon in thirds along the length

Fig. 3-24

Then apply more gluestick to the folded edge of the ribbon and fold in the remaining third of the ribbon so that the finished width of the ribbon is 3/8 inch. The woven edge covering the wire should be a slight but even distance from the fold.

13. Line up prepared ribbon along dotted line bend in "Handle Guide" at left side of basket.

NOTE: Make sure the side of the ribbon with jogged edges is facing down against the fabric.

14. Poke a pin straight into the board (through fabric and paper "Handle Guide") at the point where the bend ends and the basket handle begins. Poke an additional pin at the start of the ribbon to hold it in diagonal position.

NOTE: Ribbon must lie at an angle to block to begin. Lay the ribbon along the bend and it will be in the correct angled position.

15. Grasping working end of ribbon fold ribbon to the right from the first pin so that the folded ribbon runs along the outside handle curve. Poke the second

pin where the ribbon that is folded across meets the diagonal beginning ribbon, as shown in Fig. 3-25.

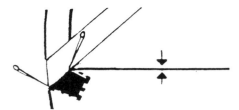

Fig. 3-25

NOTE: There should be no space between the folded corners of ribbon. Trust your eye and fold the ribbon back and forth poking a pin after each fold so that it forms a smooth curved handle between the "Handle Guides" as in Fig. 3-26. On the curves, the folds will be closer together. Folds will not be perfectly even which is fine. The handle should be the same width (3/8 inch) as it curves around.

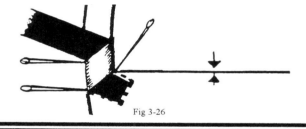

Fig 3-26

Twisted trim across basket bottom

16. Draw two parallel lines just slightly less than 3/8 inch apart across basket bottom where sides dent inward (about ¼-inch up from basket bottom). Lines are shown on "Handle Guides." (Folded ribbon will cover lines).

17. Using remaining ribbon from handle, and beginning at left side of basket bottom, lay ribbon (with woven edges face down) at angle shown by dotted lines outside basket edge.

18. Poke first pin at top where trim meets the left side of the basket as shown in Fig. 3-27.

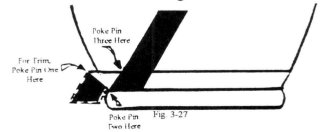

Poke Pin Three Here

For Trim Poke Pin One Here

Poke Pin Two Here

Fig. 3-27

19. Continue folding ribbon and poking pins lining up folded edge of ribbon evenly along drawn lines.

NOTE: It is easy for the ribbon to grow wider while folding and pinning so continually strive to keep the ribbon the same width, 3/8 inch.

20. To finish, pull out pins. Shift entire piece of folded trim 1/8 inch to the right so that starting fold lines up with basket edge.

21. Using wash-out fabric gluestick and a popsicle stick or toothpick, pull each pin out of handle and smooth glue between background fabric and ribbon. Put pins back in exact position to apply pressure until glue dries. Glue handle and along basket bottom trim.

22. It is fairly quick and easy to appliqué basket handle and trim in place. Using matching thread, (silk thread works wonderfully but cotton covered polyester is satisfactory as well) appliqué outer and inner edge of basket handle. Where necessary, take tiny invisible running stitches across ribbon woven edge as it runs across the handle so that handle is secured with stitches and will not move.

```
┌─────────────────────────────────────┐
│          HELPFUL HINT:                │
│ Before appliquéing handle in place, tack points │
│ together with simple stitch-and-stab stitches │
│ that draw the points together to keep the │
│ smooth curve of the handle.           │
└─────────────────────────────────────┘
```

23. Trim raw edge of ribbon that hangs past the sides of the basket on the bottom trim to within 1/8 inch of basket edge. Tuck both raw edges under and appliqué in place. Appliqué bottom trim in place like the handle.

OTHER USES FOR THIS TWIST-AND-FOLD EMBELLISHMENT:

• Monograms: Simply trace letter onto paper with dark marker trace a second line parallel to first 3/8 inch away. Fill channel with twist-and-fold embellishment;

• Trim on wearables;

• Dimensional borders on quilts or wallhangings.

STRENGTHEN THE WARM OR COOL:

Like the gentlemen in his black tuxedo and starched white shirt is to his lady in a brightly colored, sequined evening gown, so are the leaves to the flowers. The contrast between deep, lush green leaves and brightly colored flower petals is what makes flowers steal the show.

Go back to your first choice of warm and cool and choose leaves that reinforce those choices. But don't be afraid to mix things up a bit.

For instance, look at Spring's Blessing on the book cover. There is a gray background, cool blue basket and cool-toned ribbon handle. But when I auditio~~n~~ blue-toned leaves on the basket, it became borin~~g~~ was too much cool. There was no zip. Yet, when I turned to a warm leaf, the colors said "yuck." The answer was somewhere between. I found a leaf that had blue green and yellow green on it. By using this leaf, the cool colors played off the blue in the leaves and the yellow green gave a twist - some interest, but yet didn't overpower the cool theme.

DIRECTIONS:

24. To complete the basket, make nine miniature pansies from 7 mm silk ribbon using The Mini Ruching Edge. Or if you prefer, fill the basket with nine miniature mums or a mixture of many different flowers.

ENHANCE THE COLOR:

More color choices can be scary. But you've made it this far, and from now on all the color you have before you on your basket will point the way.

In considering flowers, first pick a yellow. Now some folks don't even like yellow. If you are one of those, use it in a small dose. But we must have some yellow. (I'll show you why in a little bit.) Choose between what I call "mellow yellow" — a soft yellow — or a nice bright yellow sunshine. Audition both yellows on your basket — each separately. Because yellow is one of the complementary colors in the overdyed ribbon handle, the yellow that goes with your particular piece should jump right out at you and say, ``how'd you do!"

There you've picked a flower color and it didn't hurt a bit. Now take the complement of yellow on the color wheel. That would be purple. If you are definitely not a purple person choose more of a blue violet, a neighbor of purple, if that goes with your yellow and your bas-

ket. How do you know. Move all color distractions away from your Spring's Blessing block and audition a purple or blue. If you are unsure if it is the correct tone or shade, look at the purple or blue in the overdyed ribbon - there's clues in that ribbon. When in doubt, go back to it.

A funny thing about complementary colors is that their neighbors always blend in ever so nicely. You can count on good neighbors. A good neighbor to your yellow might be orange or even red orange or yellow green. A good neighbor to purple would be red violet or blue violet. Any of these colors would make wonderful flowers in your basket.

But some variations of color are hard to work with. If all else fails, fall back on gradations of one color. To achieve a successful gradation, don't get stuck in the medium tones of a color. Find the lightest tone — a blending of white with the color. And don't dare forget the deepest, darkest shade of the color — the color mixed with black. The deepest dark and the lightest light make sense of your color gradation. They give it punch. They make it work.

ECHO COLOR:

Chances are a rush of colors have stepped forward to become flowers in your simple basket. Lay all fabric or ribbon colors you feel are working. Take yellow out of the bunch and watch what happens to the basket. It loses its life. Put the yellow in and watch all the colors peak. If possible, repeat the yellow by adding a tiny yellow bead or ruched center to a flower. It does not have to be bold. But a quiet repetition or echo of any accenting color like yellow gives the design balance.

You can use as many or as few colors as you like in your basket. The important thing is to audition each color and be an observer. Watch how the new color bounces or doesn't bounce off all the other colors. You - and the colors — then simply have to decide what you like and what you don't.

Appliqué

Starting point or use this stem to make continuous

Two **different** vines, both can be curved after cut from fabric. Both can be made continuous.

Top of vine fits into bottom of vine to make a continuous vine

Cut on true bias *from one fabric*

This vine can be curved into different shapes after cut from fabric

Add seam allowances

The Fine Art of Appliqué and Tranquility

The secret to doing beautiful appliqué lies in knowing exactly what beautiful appliqué is. In the most sterling example of appliqué, every stitch is equally and minutely spaced; every stitch is of the identical, minute length; and, every stitch is thoroughly invisible. Pristinely executed appliqué reveals nothing more than the graceful shaping of a puff of fabric mounted invisibly to a foundation fabric. Frame that puffed fabric with lines and swirls of quilting and the appliquéd shape is that much more enchanting.

What could it be that would allow a skilled hand to execute such a regular and even stitch - a stitch that almost looks mechanical in its exactness. Certainly, there are tricks to know. But once all the tricks are learned and applied, what is it that contributes to that regular and tiny of a stitch so continually perfect over the course of piece after piece in a large and intricate quilt.

The answer in one word — peace.

Talk to stitchers that have mastered the appliqué stitch and they will tell you that with that mastery has come a much higher reward.

"It's a religious experience for me," one devoted appliquér remarked. "I am quite serious. It gives me peace and serenity in my life. Without it, I shudder to think ..."

Some quilters call it their "sanity," some a "healing." Others say it gives them the sensation of floating.

They are talking about hand quilting, hand piecing, hand appliqué.

They are also describing an experience people from varying cultures and religions around the world have described similarly since the second century — the deep relaxation attained from meditation. Quilters that attain this serenity find that precise even stitches are a natural progression with the experience of relaxation.

"The quilt and I are somewhere," says Melanie Moore, a quiltmaker describing what happens when she is seated at her quilt frame at dawn in her home in

Calcutta, Ohio.

"We are in that other place. I don't know what it is, but I love it. It is so serene," she says.

"Sometimes I look up from the frame and it's 9 a.m. Some days I look up and the clock says three, and I say, `That clock has got to be wrong!'"

Melanie calls this quilting time her anchor. She says ` is mentally absent while she quilts.

"It's just me, my quilt, my thimble, and my thread. That's all that exists in that time. The roof could be on fire and I wouldn't know it, because I never look up," she says.

The serenity from hand sewing comes from being grounded only in the moment and not worrying about the past or thinking about the future, says George Bowman, a psychologist, teacher and lay Buddhist monk in Cambridge, Massachusetts.

"Thinking begins to fall away," he says. "From the Buddhist perspective, the mind becomes clear and aware and returns to its natural state, which is bright, clear and unimpeded."

Another Ohio quiltmaker, Sarah Severns of Hanoverton, describes her time spent quilting this way:

"It's almost like floating. I disconnect from the stress, the worries, the checkbook, the children. I'm in this world that I'm creating with my thimble. The world of these six stitches on my needle is all I have to think about."

Sarah, who particularly enjoys creating whole cloth quilts, calls her quilting time the center in her life.

"It's a healing process. A chance for me to put aside the upsets of the day. A time to ponder in a quiet, rational way. It lets me bring things back to mind and get a more rounded view of my feelings," she says.

Another quilter uses the relaxation effects from quilting to give her comfort while battling the pain of cancer.

"This is better than a pain-killer any day. I found piecework could shut out all this discomfort. I override the pain," she says.

Dr. Tom Kraft, a clinical psychologist with the Metropolitan Psychiatric Group in Washington, D.C., agrees that a repetitive activity like quilting can bring about a transcendental state of relaxation.

"Different kinds of activities can be used to achieve a restful or self-hypnotic state enabling one to clear the mind and focus on other things," he says.

In that restful and relaxed state, stitchers ply the needle. The hand is relaxed, the arm is relaxed and the stitches — like the thinking — are gentle and rhythmic.

Invisible Appliqué: Is It Skill Or Is It Zen?

There are many methods of appliqué. Choosing one is choosing a lifestyle. When I appliqué, I enjoy sitting in my favorite chair with my feet up watching TV with the top of my head! I don't like to iron, especially when the temperatures climb, so needleturn appliqué suits me. You have to do what you like. And quite frankly, I just want to cut that appliqué piece out one time — from the fabric only.

Appliquéing is repetitive. And it is the simplicity of the stitch and the repetition that gives me serenity. I once talked to a Buddhist monk, who said, quite simply: "It's Zen meditation."

I had no idea I was doing that, I replied.

Pulling weeds, washing dishes, repetitive activities like that, which aren't complicated, allow us to drift off and think about other things. We do a kind of mental housecleaning while we are appliquéing. We think things over ... the checkbook, what the husband said to you the night before, the kids. It's our time to mull life over. It is a steady, rhythmic experience that should be relaxing. It's no coincidence that in the 1990s, when technology is trying to push us into cramming more and more activity into each minute, appliqué offers quilters peace.

But why is that when I say needleturn appliqué, some quilters cringe?

"Doesn't work for me," they say quickly.

"Can't get those seam allowances to turn under for nothing."

I've discovered that quilters are trying to needleturn appliqué without the most important first step of fingernail pressing. In my opinion, you just can't needleturn appliqué effectively without fingernail pressing. And yet, few people talk about fingernail pressing.

Why Isn't Anyone Talking About Fingernail Pressing?

Even if you are a devoted freezer paper appliquér and never practice needleturn appliqué, knowing how to properly fingernail press will make your sewing and quilting easier.

Fingernail pressing is not just for appliqué pieces. Fingernail pressing can be used to press (without getting out of your chair!) seams, darts, hems or any little area that needs a sharp crease fast without heating up the iron. It is most effective on 100 percent cotton and some silks.

Fingernail pressing can often provide a sharper, longer lasting crease than the iron.

WHEN DO YOU FINGERNAIL PRESS?

Right after cutting out appliqué pieces, fingernail press each piece entirely before pinning in place to appliqué down. This goes for large leaves, vines of many leaves as well as tiny appliqué pieces.

HOW DO YOU FINGERNAIL PRESS?

Start with a basic almond shaped leaf. The best test of your appliqué stitch and skills is to appliqué a leaf of one color, to a background of a second color with a thread of a completely different third color! Then you'll see how invisible those stitches are.

1. Hold the appliqué piece between your thumbs and index fingers of both hands as in Fig. 4-1.

2. Tuck the seam allowance and pencil line under only in a 1/2 inch area on the sewing line.

3. Fold on the pencil line. If you fold on the pencil line, the appliqué piece will follow the graceful curves in the original pattern naturally. The pencil line will

vanish into the fold.

Fig. 4-1

4. Scrape your thumbnail across the folded edge making sure your index fingers are supporting the pressing. This helps prevent stretching but even if the sewing line is on the bias and a wavy edge results, the finished appliqué piece does not show any distortion. Don't be shy, really scrape your nails against the edge of that fabric to make a sharp crease. (Short fingernails work as well as long.)

5. Repeat for the remainder of the piece. Always fingernail press one side of a leaf first completely from point to point, then fingernail press the other side.

6. With a crisp fingerpress on 100 percent cotton, use one pin (¾-inch sequin pins work nicely) to place the piece on the background, pin in place and get ready to needleturn.

Tips For Invisible Needleturn Appliqué from A To T

APPLIQUE STITCH — This is the foundation of all appliqué.

1. Take a knot and bring the needle up through the background fabric up into the appliqué piece and out *on the fold only*.

2. The needle goes back into the background fabric just under the fold at the exact point where the previous stitch was taken in the appliqué piece. The needle advances on the back of the ground fabric and up into the fold of the appliqué piece — just 1/16 inch from the first stitch as in Fig. 4-2.

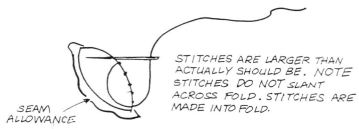

STITCHES ARE LARGER THAN ACTUALLY SHOULD BE. NOTE STITCHES DO NOT SLANT ACROSS FOLD. STITCHES ARE MADE INTO FOLD.

SEAM ALLOWANCE

Fig 4-2

3. Pull each stitch snugly and the thread will sink into the appliqué piece especially if you are appliquéing with the best thread possible — 100 percent silk (see thread in this section).

AWARD-WINNING APPLIQUE — Award-winning appliqué has no gaps where a needle or finger could pick up the piece. Points and curves are never bulky. Stitches are pulled snugly so they lay invisibly in the folds of pieces and sink into the fibers. Beautiful hand appliqué causes the appliquéd piece to puff nicely on the ground fabric but the stitches are not pulled so tight that wrinkles or puckers are created.

BASTING — Old quilts reveal that appliquérs used to baste under the seam allowance on each piece and then often again baste the piece onto the ground fabric.

Fingernail pressing eliminates basting and short appliqué or pleating pins ¾-inch long hold the piece to the background fabric and tend to not slip out. No basting please. (Unless you enjoy that kind of thing.)

CURVES — Tight curves need not be a part of appliqué that you dread. To always be able to handle inside, tight curves with grace and beauty, you need a foolproof plan. My plan is unusual, to say the least:

"Turn every curve into a straight line and fool yourself into thinking you are actually appliquéing a straight line rather than a most difficult tight curve or 'V.'"

How do you do it? Always clip curve first. Proper clipping of curves translates into well-rounded curves. On inside curves, clip right up to the penciled line as in Fig. 4-3.

The steeper the curve, the more clips needed. The more clips needed, the closer the appliqué stitches

need to be packed in to the curve. Appliqué stitches closely packed together are like cement. If you ever tried to take out close appliqué stitches you know this. Even if a curve is fraying out, it can be saved by packing appliqué stitches on top of the curve as closely as buttonhole stitches on a raw edge.

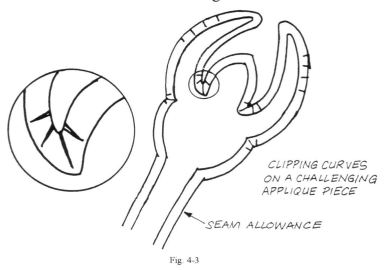

CLIPPING CURVES ON A CHALLENGING APPLIQUE PIECE

SEAM ALLOWANCE

Fig. 4-3

When appliquéing and approaching a curve as in Fig. 4-3, park your needle **and fold under and fingernail press the curve and the shape after the curve** — in this case another leaf as shown in Fig. 4-3A.

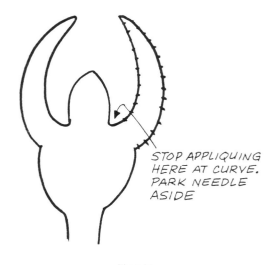

STOP APPLIQUING HERE AT CURVE. PARK NEEDLE ASIDE

Fig. 4-3A

Sew on the straight edge through the curve (Fig. 4-3B) and then pull the upcoming leaf out and continue appliquéing. It's just like appliquéing a straight line because that's what you made it!

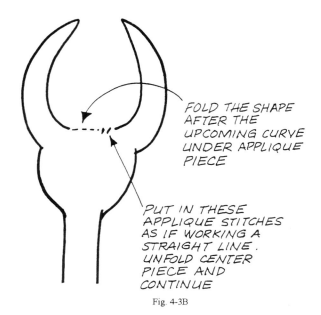

FOLD THE SHAPE AFTER THE UPCOMING CURVE UNDER APPLIQUE PIECE

PUT IN THESE APPLIQUE STITCHES AS IF WORKING A STRAIGHT LINE. UNFOLD CENTER PIECE AND CONTINUE

Fig. 4-3B

CUTTING THE GROUND FABRIC — Never cut the background fabric totally away from behind an appliqué piece. This weakens the foundation block and if there are many pieces, the entire block can fall apart. The appliqué piece puffs up more if you leave the background fabric happily in tact. You wouldn't try to remove the foundation from a house. Don't mess with the foundation block you appliqué on.

The exception is if you have to make a small opening in the ground fabric from the back to stuff a piece and will be whip stitching the opening closed.

LAYERED APPLIQUE — The most important thing to remember about layered appliqué is that you don't want bottom layers that may be dark colors showing through light-colored top layers. Judges take points off for this. This is a common problem with flowers. Dark green stems often show through light yellow flowers.

Avoid this situation by placing either a piece of batting behind the light-colored appliqué piece or another piece of fabric the same color. I like to use batting.

LEAF POINTS — First, always lay a leaf so seam allowances at the point fall on the bias. That will insure that curves lie on the bias and will be smoother and easier to appliqué. Of course, if you are trying to capture a particular color on printed fabric, that rule gets thrown out the window! Go for color first.

The most important thing to remember about making sharp appliquéd points on leaf tips is to take your very last appliqué stitch right in the very end of the tip of the point. This means the marked point and not the raw edge. If you stop short of the very tip, the point will not be sharp.

Once one side of the point is sewed, its time to trim away any excess layers of fabric that add bulk. It is important to do this because when an iron hits a bulky point it creates shine. Also in the long run, bulky points will wear out first.

I trim my leaf point right after I sew the first side of the leaf. You can also trim straight across the point very close to the leaf tip and then taper both seam allowances before pinning leaf in place.

Once trimmed, needleturn the other side of the point under and appliqué.

NEEDLETURNING:

1. Fingernail press carefully the section where you wish to begin.

2. Bring the knot up from the back of the background fabric.

3. Using the tip of the needle tuck the seam allowance under on already fingernail pressed fold. The needle simply urges the seam allowance under. The needle also can be used to pull out a seam allowance to fill out a curve that may be too straight.

POINTS — Under any point there should be only one or two layers of seam allowance. Cut the third or more layers away before you get to it. Sometimes this means trimming dangerously close to the sewing line, but do it anyway! Just put stitches closer together at the dangerous spot.

How to get rid of points when you really wanted curves — If you are getting points rather than graceful curves, there are three possible mistakes you may be making:

1. You are traveling too great a distance between stitches;

2. You are needleturning too far ahead of where you are stitching;

3. The seam allowance is too big and is folding creating points at the appliqué edge.

PRACTICE — Appliqué is a skill that requires practice.

SEAM ALLOWANCE — Add a 3/16-inch seam allowance or even as little as 1/8 inch if the fabric is tightly woven and not fraying badly as you cut the appliqué piece out of the fabric. If the seam allowance is too wide, points will result where you want smooth curves.

TANGLED APPLIQUE THREAD — Often while appliquéing the thread regularly tangles. Every time a stitch is taken, the needle is often twisted one way or another. Rather than stopping your stitching, and turning your work upside down to untangle the needle and thread, take a stitch this way. As soon as you can feel the thread beginning to tangle as you stitch:

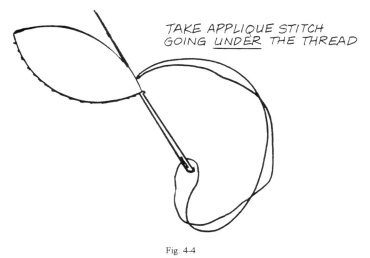

TAKE APPLIQUE STITCH
GOING _UNDER_ THE THREAD

Fig. 4-4

Take the next appliqué stitch into the background fabric by going under the thread that is coming out of the appliqué piece as shown in Fig. 4-4. Normally, when we take the stitch, the thread hangs in front of the appliqué piece and the stitch is taken over the thread. To untangle, begin the appliqué stitch by going under the arched thread.

THREAD — I highly recommend using silk thread on all fine appliqué - it just makes the work so much easier. And if your stitch isn't perfect, it covers it up! It is even easier to thread the small eye of a needle with silk thread. The fine silk thread actually sinks into the coarser cotton fibers. Since silk thread is more expensive many appliquérs choose a neutral color like light gray for all appliqué patches. The silk sinks in so superbly it isn't even necessary to match the color of the thread exactly.

My second choice of thread is 100 percent cotton. From a textile conservationist viewpoint, the textile will endure well if you use cotton on cotton. Cotton thread requires waxing since it tangles and frays easily.

Cotton-covered polyester seems to be most easily available and would be a third choice if silk and cotton were not available.

If not using silk thread to appliqué, matching the color of the thread to the color of the appliqué is very important. If your stitch is not perfect, this can cover up a multitude of sins. Always choose thread that is slightly darker than the fabric. Lighter thread will show more.

The Three-Dimensional Swag Border

*(For The Enchanted Garden,
a nine-block wallhanging)*

Add a new dimension to the traditional swag border seen on album quilts with this revolutionary and fast method.

MATERIALS:

NOTE: When cutting borders, cut two at one time — the straight, flat background border and the 3-D swag border.

• Four strips cut 18¾ inches by 4 inches for swags

• Four strips cut 28 inches by 4 inches for border background behind swags

• Four 1¼-inch squares in a fabric that coordinates with swags

NOTE: To border other size wallhangings and quilts with the 3-D swag border, cut border background strips as usual. Cut swags the exact length as edge of blocks to be bordered plus ½ inch (for folded under seam allowances) by four inches wide.

DIRECTIONS:

1. On each swag piece, fold under ¼ inch on three sides and press. Do not press under on one of the longest sides.

2. Sew the double borders to quilt blocks this way: With right sides together, first lay the unpressed edge of swag rectangular fabric piece onto quilt blocks making sure swag piece extends the length of the quilt blocks plus ¼ inch on each end.

3. Next, lay the next right side of border centered and facedown on top of swag piece, lining up raw edges.

4. Pin double border to quilt blocks.

5. Machine sew all borders on — through all three layers — with a ¼-inch seam allowance right to the very edge of the quilt blocks.

6. Press seams open.

7. Open wallhanging and borders so right sides are facing upward on table.

8. Draw chalk lines straight out across top swag borders from seams lines as shown in Fig. 5-1.

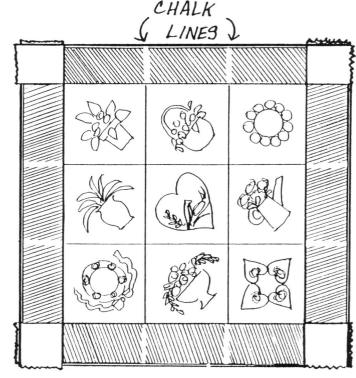

Fig. 5-1

9. Using a doubled, matching thread, hand gather on chalk lines as shown from outer most edge *of swag border only* toward seam where borders are attached to quilt.

NOTE: Only gather through top border. Pull gathers as tight as possible. Double knot for extra security. Repeat on all chalk lines and hand gather also down folds at sides. These gathers will form swags, as in Fig. 5-2.

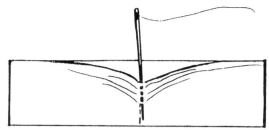

HAND GATHER
ON CHALK LINES
THROUGH TOP
FABRIC **ONLY**

Fig. 5-2

10. Miter the four corners of the background border.

11. Smooth out background border on a table first. Next, machine sew with matching thread right across the top of gathers *through background borders* allowing machine stitches to sink into gathers and making sure swag fabric remains folded under on outer edge. Back tack.

NOTE: Sew across gathers on inner gathers first and then sew the gathers down at the corners making sure to pull the gathers toward corners to help swag form into a shape similar to inner swags.

12. Cut four 1¼-inch squares from a fabric that coordinates with swag borders for the squares that will cover edges of swags at corners.

13. Fingerpress the ¼-inch seam allowance under on all sides of each square. Hand applique squares in place making sure edges of gathers are tucked under squares and appliqued in place. Lay a bit of batting behind each square before completely appliqueing square in place.

14. The pleats on each swag are meant to be random — not perfect — almost as if each swag was a curtain pulled back on a stage. With that in mind, take a hot iron and press random pleats into each swag in this way:

A. To begin arranging folds, first again fingerpress the folded fabric at the outer curve of swag so the fold is crisp.

B. Pull out that outer most edge of swag so that swag takes on a nicely arched shape. Trust your eye to make sure all swags have a similar curve.

C. Smooth out the background border as you shape each arch and then pin outermost edge of swag in place.

D. Leave 5/8-inch space from seam where the swag joins the quilt blocks to the first pleat. Add two more pleats. Set all the pleats with the iron, as in Fig. 5-3.

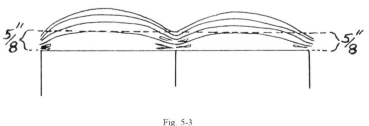

Fig. 5-3

15. Pin the rounded outer edge of each swag in place on background border.

16. Applique each swag outer edge in place. Applique or invisibly tack folds in place as desired.

Favorite Miniature 3-Band Seminole Border

(For The Garden Sampler, a four-block wallhanging)

1. Choose three fabrics that graduate light to dark for border in colors that coordinate with blocks. **NOTE:** Two different color schemes can be used for a border half one color on two sides, half the other color on two sides as shown in the four-block wallhanging The Garden Sampler.

2. Cut strips:

- lightest fabric 1 inch by 80 inches

- medium fabric 5/8 inch by 80 inches

- dark fabric 1 inch by 80 inches

NOTE: Split above measurements in half if using two-color border

3. Sew light fabric to medium fabric with a 1/8-inch seam allowance down length. Press seam toward medium fabric.

4. Sew dark fabric to medium fabric with a 1/8-inch seam allowance down length. Press seam toward medium fabric.

5. Press sewed strips flat.

6. With rotary cutter, cut sewn strip in 1 inch pieces as shown in Fig. 5-4.

7. Jog each piece and sew with a ¼-inch-seam allowance as shown in Fig. 5-5.

8. Trim off points on both edges along the line formed where raw edge V's form as in Fig. 5-5.

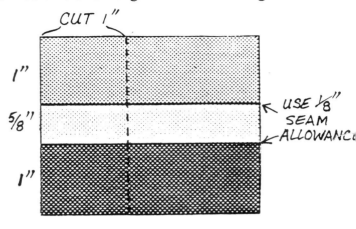

Fig. 5-4

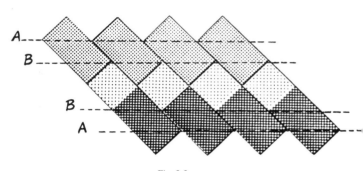

Fig. 5-5

NOTE: A = Cutting Line   B = Seam Line

9. Sew borders onto wallhanging using a ¼-inch seam allowance.

10. The corners on this border are a challenge. Allow a seam to lie on each mitered corner. However, if you don't care for the look of the patches or colors as they come together on the corner, appliqué in a compensating piece where needed.

About the author

Cindy is a writer by trade. But she has always found solace in working with her hands. When seven years old, her Auntie Marie taught her how to pick up a crochet hook and do the simple chain stitch. She chain stitched miles. As a young Girl Scout, she was again encouraged to work with her hands making all those fun crafts in the 1960s. She felt that as a young child if she were ever bored or lonely, she could always create with her hands, occupy her mind and find peace.

``The women I knew and admired as a child all sewed,'' she recalled. Her Aunt Lil was a jovial woman who always had sewing on the machine, sewn dolls and other projects to show and a big plate of homemade brownies on the table when she arrived for a visit. While playing at a friend's house, she would occasionally walk through the well-kept livingroom and gaze at a huge, intricately embroidered crewel work canvas. A Hungarian woman up the street did alterations and kept a fascinating round rack of hand sewn clothing for sale that she would admire.

``I had a fabulous home economics teacher when I was going to junior high in Cleveland, Ruth L. Meyer. She was extremely strict. She made us keep meticulous sewing notebooks documenting every kind of buttonhole and seam. At the time, I couldn't imagine how grateful I would be for that someday,'' Cindy recalls.

As a junior high school student, she received her first sewing machine - a Morse that sewed forward and backwards. When her chores were done, she could go to her basement sewing room and create and sew outfits as long as she liked. Polyester had just come into fashion. She and The Morse produced many high-

Cindy Zlotnik Oravecz

waisted plaid pants and coordinating blazers. As she sat on the floor laying out her patterns, her Airedale, Tootse, would lay with his head on her lap. ``He was a great sewing buddy and he never walked on the patterns.''

College found her embroidering her blue jeans and peasant tops madly. She had a hippie friend that made the warmest blue jean quilts backed with red flannel and who also let Cindy sew on her machine.

After college, Cindy plunged into journalism. As a police reporter, the violence that she was forced to witness on a day to day basis was shocking to her. ``I'd run home to my sewing machine and only think about that needle going in and out of the fabric. It grounded me and brought me peace.''

With the birth of her first child and the desire to be a home Mom, Cindy began freelance writing. Like a light bulb turning on, she thought, since I love sewing so much what am I doing writing about sewer assessments, politics and death. She wrote her first sewing article. ``Or rather, it wrote itself,'' she says.

Her motto, ``Follow your heart, and you'll find the work you love. And you'll be one of those people that love what they do. That's a good way to spend your life.

``Looking back on how sewing touched my childhood, I feel we must pass on our traditions of creating with our hands to our children. Any chance you get, teach a child the love of sewing.''

Today, Cindy enjoys teaching her three-dimensional flower making techniques and meeting stitchers from everywhere.

Resources

One of the elements that made the album quilts of Baltimore so spectacular was the port city itself. At the middle of the 19th century the most diverse textiles from all over the world were pouring into that bustling port. Those quilt makers had a vast array of spectacular textiles to create the album blocks.

The success of the album blocks of today relies on wonderful goods as well. That is why Quilter's Fancy offers a range of hard-to-find products designed for album quilts.

You'll find the complete palette of French Elegance wired ribbon, variegated silk ribbons, silk fabrics as well as the best needles and notions tested and recommended by Quilter's Fancy available by mail.

All of the materials needed for *Into The Enchanted Garden* & related patterns and tools for three-dimensional appliqué are available by mail order from:

P.O. Box 457
Cortland, Ohio 44410 U.S.A.
To order call Toll-Free 1-800-484-7944 code 7673
Fax your order to 330-637-3106
Call or write for a free catalogue

Teaching Seminars Available. Write or call for packet.

Have you tried Cindy's other products?

• The Ruching Edge
• The book: Into The Garden, Realistic 3-D Flowers Faster By The Strip
• 60 Leaves on Heat Resistant Templar (from Into The Garden)
• 60 Leaves on Freezer Paper (from Into The Garden)
• The Mini Ruching Edge
• The Three-Dimensional Pansy & Viola pattern (available in the book Into The Garden) or separately

ISBN 0-9652160-1-2

90000